The Launch Pad!

COPYRIGHT© Maxime Du Pont 2017

Smartwellness Launch pad on YouTube

Are you ready?! Because your life is about to drastically improve!

The Smartwellness Launch Pad launches you into a creative and positive mind-set using various scientifically proven techniques, which include Self-Affirmations, Visualizations, fabricated Laughter and wellness enhancement facts. This is one of the easiest paths to reach your optimal wellness. Rather than spending decades trying to create your own path, I have cleared the path for you. You will quickly transition into the fitter, smarter and happier you!

The smart wellness Launch Pad includes 90+ days of ultra-super wellness reprogramming material. It is broken down between Laughter days and Regular days (morning portion and evening portion).

Laughter and Love Meditation days

Every few days, you have a laughter and love kindness meditation day. On those days, there are no self-affirmations or wellness facts. It is a day where you focus on laughter and use your imagination to feel, experience, and send your love to someone else.

Your imagination is extremely powerful. As it turns out, just by imagining things and immersing yourself, you can trigger substantial physical benefits. In fact, athletes have known this for a while, which is why you will see basketball players and golf pros visualize their free-throws or putts beforehand.

1. "Love kindness meditation [visualization focused] enhanced a wide range of positive emotions in a wide range of situations, especially when interacting with others. We find these data especially promising. LKM appears to be one positive emotion induction that keeps on giving, long after the identifiable "event" of meditation practice."

   https://www.ncbi.nlm.nih.gov/pmc/articles/PMC3156028/

2. "The use of mental techniques to strengthen mental toughness is well accepted for professional athletes at times of championships. In professional sports competitions, different mental techniques such as progressive muscle relaxation techniques, breathing techniques, autogenic training, hypnosis, biofeedback, and visualization have been shown to be able to improve the mental skills of professional athletes."

   https://www.ncbi.nlm.nih.gov/pubmed/27172777

3. The present review also indicates advantageous effects of internal imagery (range from 2.6 to 136.3%) for strength performance compared with external imagery (range from 4.8 to 23.2%).

   https://www.ncbi.nlm.nih.gov/pmc/articles/PMC4974856/

Finally, you must vividly imagine and thank the universe ahead of time for granting you an amazing wish. For example, "thank you, universe for bringing 1 million YouTube subscribers to my smart wellness channel!!!"

Regular days

You will start your fantastic day in the morning by performing fabricated laughter, appreciation, and self-affirmations. Your morning will be followed by a vibrating evening of learning wellness enabling facts, performing acknowledgements and expressing a motivation quote or joke.

The Morning portion of a regular day consists of,

- Laughing for 10 seconds.
- Completing two "I am thankful" statements.
- Completing two self-affirmation statements.
- Enumerating the important tasks of the day, that if completed, will make you feel satisfied.

The Evening portion of a regular day consists of,

- Acknowledging a super whole food you ate during the day.
- Answering between 1-3 wellness enhancing questions, Or re-copying a wellness enhancing statement. Don't stress out trying to answer the questions, just answer your best guess. The point of the questions is to get you to think a little bit about things that can impact your health.
- Acknowledging three fantastic things that happened during the day.
- Acknowledging one reason why you laughed during the day.
- Plan how you will enhance your wellness for the next day.
- A motivating quote or joke to help put a smile on your face.

Fabricated laughter

Do you remember the last time you laughed your ass off? Do you have a memorable laugh? Here's the sensational news, you're about to become someone with an amazing laugh!

Laughter is the cheapest and quickest method to get well, reduce stress, and become creative and positive. However, it may be difficult for you to find a reason to laugh. But here's the thing, you don't need to have a comedian in front of you or hear a really funny joke to laugh. You can simulate or fabricate your laughter. This is also known as laughter yoga; I am a certified laughter yoga leader. Laughter yoga is simply laughing combined with breathing. The benefits of simulated laughter and real laughter are extremely similar if not practically the same.

Every single day, the new and improved you will pretend to laugh for 10 seconds. The new you will do this, because pretending to laugh for 10 seconds or more will reduce your stress and make you happy. Your moto will change from, "I laugh because it's funny" to "I'm happy because I laugh." Moreover, the more you exercise your laughter muscles through fabricated laughter, the better your laugh will become and the more you will laugh for real.

- Fabricated laughter lowers the stress hormone cortisol. It improves the signs of physical and sleep disorders, lowers anxiety and depression, and promotes social function.

  https://www.ncbi.nlm.nih.gov/pmc/articles/PMC3917183/

- "Chronic Stress impacts Limbic system and Hypothalamus continuously and leads to Adrenaline secretion and causes disruption in immune system. Indeed, Laughter balances sympathetic and parasympathetic system; moreover, it functions as an anti-stress. Furthermore, laughter increases endorphins in brain. Endorphins seem to be the most easily linked structure to morphine, both function in the exhilaration and lessening of pain."

  https://www.ncbi.nlm.nih.gov/pmc/articles/PMC4307100/

Gratitude

The power of gratitude cannot be understated. Perhaps you have heard of Albert Einstein's quote, "you cannot solve problems with the same mindset that created them." According to the Kabbalah, the universe has both creative (Gedulah) and destructive (Geburah) forces. To start-up your creative powers, there is nothing easier than jumping on the appreciation, laughter and self-affirmations trampolines.

You will write, "I, your name, am thankful for XXX because of XXX."

Examples

- "I, Maxime Du Pont, am thankful for my little dog Edward because he makes me smile."
- "I, Maxime Du Pont, am thankful for the sandwich my girlfriend made me because I have something to eat."
- "I, Maxime Du Pont, am thankful for my friends, because they are encouraging."

Use your full or formal name: Yes, you can write just your first name. However, I have noticed that by using my full name, just like when someone says your full name, it becomes much more formal and powerful, which I believe will lead to greater accountability. For example, Max has decided to change his life versus Max Du Pont has decided to change his life.

Use justifications: The word "because" is extremely powerful to get people to do stuff. In fact, in the landmark study by ELLEN J. LANGER, the difference between being permitted to skip the line was 30% greater if the person provided a reason or justification, even if the reason was not meaningful.

- "Excuse me, I have 5 pages. May I use the xerox machine?" [60% compliance]
- "Excuse me, I have 5 pages. May I use the xerox machine, because I have to make copies?" [93% compliance]
- "Excuse me, I have 5 pages. May I use the xerox machine, because I'm in a rush?" [94% compliance]

You do not have to break your head to come with the ideal justification. If you can't come up with anything, you can simple say "I am thankful for xxx, because I am thankful" or "I am thankful for xxx, because I am happy."

Self-affirmations

Do you know that you are a fantastic person? Well, if you didn't, you're about to find out using self-affirmations! Self-affirmations are as simple as saying "I am great, I am super, and I am smart." Although it seems simple, most people, including myself, don't actually use these words to describe themselves in their own minds on a daily basis. Instead, they actually use very negative language. Language that does not support them, but actually damages them. For example, "I'm fat, I'm stupid, I'm really going to suck, I'm crap, nobody loves me..."

As part of every single day, you will get a new empowering and enhancing adjective. For example, you will write, "I, Maxime Du Pont, am sexy, because I have an amazing laugh." The reason you come up with, should hopefully be true, but it doesn't have to be. However, the reason should be positive, you should not sabotage yourself, and say something like "I, Maxime Du Pont, am sexy, because I have an ugly smile."

- Self-affirmations "increase activity in the ventromedial prefrontal cortex." *https://www.ncbi.nlm.nih.gov/pubmed/25646442*
- "Deploying self-affirmation inductions alongside persuasive health information has positive effects, promoting message acceptance, intentions to change, and subsequent behavior." *https://www.ncbi.nlm.nih.gov/pubmed/25133846*

Socioemotional wellness enhancing information

At the time of this writing, I still eat meat, although it is mostly composed of non-hormone non-antibiotic organic meat...

I recently met an abs of steel muscular vegetarian guy named Pat while I was walking my dog, Edward. We spoke for a good hour, during which we spoke about veganism, animals and fasting. But, what I found astonishing, about Pat, was how he was surprised that extremely smart people were eating crap food and meat. He, for example, could not understand how his professor of evolutionary psychology, that he found extremely rational and intelligent, was at the same time fat and ate an extremely poor diet.

To me of course, this isn't surprising at all. Just because you're extremely smart or intelligent or knowledgeable in one subject or sphere, doesn't necessarily translate to another subject or sphere. Just because you know everything about cars, doesn't translate to you knowing whole bunch about vegetables. Just because you know a lot about politics, doesn't mean you know anything about exercise. Just because you are a medical doctor with 30 years of experience, doesn't actually mean you have more than a rudimentary understanding of nutrients.

The other thing that Pat didn't notice when I was speaking with him was that I was very conscious, that just by speaking to him for an hour would help me reprogram my mind to take steps to becoming a vegan and eating less meat. There is nothing more powerful than having a conversation with someone who is extremely fit, strong and knowledgeable and leading by example to help you change. When you see someone like Pat, there's no way you can say vegans are weak and scrawny, and so the excuse of not being a vegan because it'll make me weak is definitely not valid.

In another related note, what's the difference between a hockey fan and a football fan? Why is the hockey fan not a football fan? Now, some of you might think some people just don't like hockey and some people just love football. However, the real question is, why do you ever start to like a thing or a sport in this case? I am definitely not a fan of watching CFL football or sports that are not hockey. The reason I'm not a fan of football, is that I have not consumed enough quality football social emotional information. I did not have a father that watched football, and I did not play football as a child. As a result, I did not share any worthwhile positive emotional experience in my childhood revolving football.

However, hockey is Canada's most popular sport. Hockey is a way to socialize with other Canadians, other than talking about the weather. Coworkers might say, "Did you see the game last night?" I became a true fan of hockey and the Canadiens in high school, because everyone was talking about it, especially my friend Russell Stewart and William Descotes. In fact, Russel and I skipped school to purchase playoff tickets to see the Canadiens beat the Boston Bruins. Since then and unfortunately, I have spent over 10K on Canadiens related items like tickets and spent at least 10 hours a week consuming Canadiens and hockey related information. Some people might call me a fanatic, and maybe that's true because I do not make my income via hockey. In fact, I've never actually played in a hockey game, because I cannot skate.

So, what's the difference between a fanatic and someone who is completely indifferent about a thing? It is simply quality social emotional information. So, if you want to change, the most effective and efficient way to do so, is to overload yourself with quality social and emotional information. This means, you must immerse yourself with people doing the thing you would like to do, learning and taking notes about the thing you want to do. I can almost guarantee to you, that if you had to kill, slaughter, skin, debone, and butcher a cow yourself, it is highly unlikely you would eat a burger right after. You might even become a vegetarian. All because you went through an extreme experience, by today's standards.

The facts in this launch pad and recommended videos will re-calibrate your mind for wellness success, but it will not happen overnight. However, the more factual and quality social emotional facts you have about nutrition, toxins, and exercise, the more likely you are to take steps to implementing and using that information to enhance your well-being!

Using facts and answering questions

You do not have to break your head to find the answers to the questions. The answers to all true and false questions are true. The answers to how much nutrient there is in any question, is always the most. I highly recommend that whenever you see a question or a fact, try to put it into your own words or remember the keywords and repeat them in your mind, because doing so will integrate that information much quicker into your mind and lead to a more enhancing nutrient dense and toxin-free life.

Videos+Podcast

Please consume wellness related videos and podcasts if you want to speed up your wellness enhancement process. I also highly recommend that you find your own videos to watch and you note them down in this book. You will note down the date, the title of the video, the subject matter, the duration of the video, and one or three takeaways from the video. I highly recommend before you start watching any of these videos, you find yourself a clipboard, put a blank piece of paper on it, and write down the information that would allow you to teach someone about what was in that video. The most important thing is that you have fun doing this; this isn't supposed to be stressful, it's supposed to be a much easier way to get you well. What this means is that if you're not up to taking notes, and you just feel like watching five minutes of a video, then that is still amazing! Every bit counts, you do not need to do everything at 100% to get valuable benefits, because just 2% everyday over a period of 50 days can also give you 100%!   Start by **Subscribing yourself to my YouTube channel, "Smart Wellness."**

Other videos to get you started: Type in the title of the video in Google and you should find it.

1. Jamie Oliver: Teach every child about food
2. Dan Buettner: How to live to be 100+
3. Unprocessed -- how I gave up processed foods (and why it matters) | Megan Kimble
4. Reversing Type 2 diabetes starts with ignoring the guidelines | Sarah Hallberg | TEDxPurdueU
5. Dan Barber: How I fell in love with a fish
6. Jennifer 8. Lee: The hunt for General Tso
7. Birke Baehr: What's wrong with our food system
8. Ben Goldacre: What doctors don't know about the drugs they prescribe
9. Russ Altman: What really happens when you mix medications?
10. Unblind My Mind: What are we eating?: Dr. Katherine Reid at TEDxYouth@GrassValley
11. Your ecosystem on MSG: Katherine L. Reid at TEDxSantaCruz
12. Why some people find exercise harder than others | Emily Balcetis | TEDxNewYork

The Videos you have watched

Example

1.Date: May 5/17 Title: Sitting will kill you, even if you exercise Sub: Movement   Time:1 min

Takeaway: Move when sitting to improve circulation, humans are not made to sit .

2.Date:_____Title:_____Sub:_____Time:_____

Takeaway:_____

_____

3.Date:_____Title:_____Sub:_____Time:_____

Takeaway:_____

_____

 4.Date:_____Title:_____Sub:_____Time:_____

Takeaway:_____

_____

5.Date:_____Title:_____Sub:_____Time:_____

Takeaway:_____

_____

6.Date:_____Title:_____Sub:_____Time:_____

Takeaway:_____

_____

7.Date:_____Title:_____Sub:_____Time:_____

Takeaway:_____

8.Date:_____Title:_____Sub:_____Time:____

Takeaway:_____

_____

9.Date:_____Title:_____Sub:_____Time:____

Takeaway:_____

_____

10.Date:_____Title:_____Sub:_____Time:___

Takeaway:_____

_____

11.Date:_____Title:_____Sub:_____Time:___

Takeaway:_____

_____

12.Date:_____Title:_____Sub:_____Time:___

Takeaway:_____

_____

13.Date:_____Title:_____Sub:_____Time:___

Takeaway:_____

_____

14.Date:_____Title:_____Sub:_____Time:___

Takeaway:_____

_____

15.Date:_____Title:_____Sub:_____Time:___

Takeaway:_____

_____

16.Date:_____Title:_____Sub:_____Time:___

Takeaway:_____

_____

17.Date:_____Title:_____Sub:_____Time:___

Takeaway:_____

_____

18.Date:_____Title:_____Sub:_____Time:___

Takeaway:_____

_____

19.Date:_____Title:_____Sub:_____Time:___

Takeaway:_____

_____

20.Date:_____Title:_____Sub:_____Time:____

Takeaway:_____

_____

21.Date:_____Title:_____Sub:_____Time:____

Takeaway:_____

_____

22.Date:_____Title:_____Sub:_____Time:____

Takeaway:_____

_____

23.Date:_____Title:_____Sub:_____Time:____

Takeaway:_____

_____

24.Date:_____Title:_____Sub:_____Time:____

Takeaway:_____

_____

25.Date:_____Title:_____Sub:_____Time:____

Takeaway:_____

_____

26.Date:_____Title:_____Sub:_____Time:___

Takeaway:_____

_____

27.Date:_____Title:_____Sub:_____Time:___

Takeaway:_____

_____

28.Date:_____Title:_____Sub:_____Time:___

Takeaway:_____

_____

29.Date:_____Title:_____Sub:_____Time:___

Takeaway:_____

_____

30.Date:_____Title:_____Sub:_____Time:___

Takeaway:_____

_____

31.Date:_____Title:_____Sub:_____Time:___

Takeaway:_____

_____

32.Date:_____Title:_____Sub:_____Time:___

Takeaway:_____

_____

33.Date:_____Title:_____Sub:_____Time:___

Takeaway:_____

_____

34.Date:_____Title:_____Sub:_____Time:___

Takeaway:_____

_____

35.Date:_____Title:_____Sub:_____Time:___

Takeaway:_____

_____

36.Date:_____Title:_____Sub:_____Time:___

Takeaway:_____

_____

37.Date:_____Title:_____Sub:_____Time:___

Takeaway:_____

_____

How to find studies to help you further overload your mind.

Finding studies is fairly straightforward. All you have to do is type the keywords you're looking for in Google, followed by NBCI. And NCBI stands for, The National Centre for Biotechnology Information. So, if you're looking for effects of how exercise increases the size of your brain, or if zinc increases testosterone, then all you have to do is type in specific keywords that should lead you to finding those studies. For example, in Google, type in "zinc testosterone NCBI." Now, keep in mind whatever you type in, you will find. Keep in mind however, that there are multiple ways to describe a thing, for example "vitamin C" is also known as "ascorbic acid," and can lead to two very different set of results. Also, if you type in "vitamin C liver," it will obviously give you different results than typing in "vitamin C brain NCBI."

Helpful questions to enhance your well-being

1. How do I feel after 7 days of not consuming sugar, fried-food and alcohol?
2. How do I feel after 7 days of consuming 30 g of fiber or glutamine daily?
3. Do I feel energized or smarter after eating or tired?
4. How do I feel after 7 days of consuming only water after 6PM?
5. Do I poo twice a day? Do I know the difference between a good poo and bad poo?
6. How would I feel after 7 days of only drinking carbonated spring water?
7. Do I spend more than 3 minutes pooing? Could I imagine my dog or cat taking more than 3 minutes squatting to poo?
8. What would happen, if I ate everything I wanted during the day for lunch and breakfast, but ate only veggies at night and drank water?
9. What would happen to my LDL cholesterol if I took 1 gram of Niacin every day for 3 months?
10. How is my poo after a night of heavy drinking or sugar binging?
11. If normal means being fat and anxious and having no libido, do I really want to be normal?
12. What if today, I only ate foods that I could actually make from scratch, what would I eat?
13. How would I feel after 30 days of turning-off the WI-FI before going to bed?
14. How would it feel, if I smiled and laughed during every single one of my interactions this week?
15. How would you feel after 30 days of consuming the intake of vitamins and minerals recommended by your government?
16. If it took 50 years for the government to warn me about tobacco, do I really want to put my life in the hands of the government?

<u>Laughter Day!</u>

Pretend to laugh for 10 seconds!

Visualize a family member or close friend Smiling and Laughing

Visualize a colleague Smiling and Laughing

Visualize someone you don't know Smiling and Laughing

Pretend to laugh for 10 seconds

Thank you, Universe, for?

<u>NOTES</u>

Pretend to Laugh for 10 seconds :)!!!

I am Thankful

1.   I, _____, am_____ for_____,

because_____

2.   I, _____, am_____ for_____,

because_____

I am Super

1. I, _____, am_____

because_____

2. I, _____, am_____

because_____

Most important tasks of the day?

1._____

2._____

I ate this enhancing super whole food

☐ Carrots ☐ Apple ☐ Cucumber ☐ Other_____

Nutrition

Vitamin D Experts recommend how much vitamin D?
☐ 50 IU ☐ 500 IU ☐ 1000IU ☐ Over 3000 IU

Studies have proven that intake of 5000IU of vitamin D increases the aerobic capacity and speed of athletes, and puts inflammatory bowel disease and Crohn's into remission in 24 weeks. TRUE OR FALSE_____

The most abundant source of Vitamin D is?
☐ Salmon ☐ Sardines ☐ Tuna ☐ Eggs

I Acknowledge

Three fantastic things that happened today?

1._____

2._____

3._____

I laughed or smiled today because

_____

How will I enhance tomorrow?

_____

"To accomplish great things, we must not only act, but also dream, not only plan, but also believe." - Anatole France

Pretend to Laugh for 10 seconds :)!!!

I am Thankful

1. I, _____, am_____ for_____,

because_____

2. I, _____, am_____ for_____,

because_____

I am Rich

1. I, _____, am_____

because_____

2. I, _____, am_____

because_____

Most important tasks of the day?

1._____

2._____

I ate this enhancing super whole food

☐ Carrots ☐ Apple ☐ Cucumber ☐ Other_____

Nutrition

The daily recommend intake of fiber for a 40-year-old man is?
☐ 2 grams ☐ 5 grams ☐ 13 grams ☐ 35 grams

An average apple contains how many grams of fiber?

☐ 500mg ☐ 1 g ☐ 7 g ☐ 3 g

I Acknowledge

Three fantastic things that happened today?

1._____

2._____

3._____

I laughed or smiled today because

_____

How will I enhance tomorrow?

_____

*"Great works are performed not by strength,
but perseverance." - Dr. Samuel Johnson*

Pretend to Laugh for 10 seconds :)!!!

I am Thankful

1. I, _____, am_____ for_____,

because_____

2. I, _____, am_____ for_____,

because_____

I am Very Attractive

1. I, _____, am_____

because_____

2. I, _____, am_____

because_____

Most important tasks of the day?

1._____

2._____

I ate this enhancing super whole food

☐ Carrots ☐ Broccoli ☐ Cucumber ☐ Other_____

Nutrition

The daily recommend intake of Potassium for an adult is?
☐ 15 mg ☐ 25 mg ☐ 100 mg ☐ 4700 mg

Potassium neutralizes acidity in the bloodstream?
TRUE OR FALSE? _____

Potassium supplementation is scientifically proven to reduce blood pressure?
TRUE OR FALSE? _____

What has the least potassium?

☐ Beet Greens 1309 mg ☐ Spinach 800mg ☐ Broccoli 500 mg ☐ Bananas 400 mg

I Acknowledge

Three fantastic things that happened today?

1._____

2._____

3._____

I laughed or smiled today because

_____

How will I enhance tomorrow?

_____

**"To be a leader, you must stand for something,
or you will fall for anything."**
- Anthony Pagano

Laughter Day!

Pretend to laugh for 10 seconds!

Visualize a family member or close friend Smiling and Laughing

Visualize a colleague Smiling and Laughing

Visualize someone you don't know Smiling and Laughing

Pretend to laugh for 10 seconds

Thank you, Universe, for?

NOTES

Pretend to Laugh for 10 seconds :)!!!

I am Thankful

1. I, _____, am_____ for_____,

   because_____

2. I, _____, am_____ for_____,

   because_____

I am Hilarious

1. I, _____, am_____

because_____

2. I, _____, am_____

because_____

Most important tasks of the day?

1._____

2._____

I ate this enhancing super whole food

☐ Cabbage ☐ Apple ☐ Cucumber ☐ Other_____

Sleep

The optimal sleeping position to eliminate toxins from your brain is on your stomach? TRUE or FALSE? _____

The vast majority of brain detoxification happens during sleep? TRUE OR FALSE? _____

I Acknowledge

Three fantastic things that happened today?

1._____

2._____

3._____

I laughed or smiled today because

_____

How will I enhance tomorrow?

_____

**"If we are to achieve results never before accomplished,
we must expect to employ methods never before attempted." - Francis Bacon**

Pretend to Laugh for 10 seconds :)!!!

I am Thankful

1. I, _____, am_____ for_____,

    because_____

2. I, _____, am_____ for_____,

    because_____

I am Intelligent

1. I, _____, am_____

because_____

2. I, _____, am_____

because_____

Most important tasks of the day?

1._____

2._____

I ate this enhancing super whole food

☐ Carrots ☐ Lentils ☐ Cucumber ☐ Other_____

Nutrition

The daily recommend intake of phosphorus for an adult is?
☐ 15 mg ☐ 25 mg ☐ 100 mg ☐ 700 mg

Phosphorus is critical for bone formation and energy (ATP) production? TRUE OR FALSE? _____

Phosphorus supplementation (500 mg) is scientifically proven to reduce waist circumference?
TRUE OR FALSE? _____

Have you eaten a food with abundant phosphorous this week?

☐ Pumpkin Seeds ☐ Crimini mushroom ☐ Cod ☐ Lentils

I Acknowledge

Three fantastic things that happened today?

1._____

2._____

3._____

I laughed or smiled today because

_____

How will I enhance tomorrow?

_____

**"I have tried 99 times and have failed,
but on the 100th time came success." - Albert Einstein**

Pretend to Laugh for 10 seconds :)!!!

I am Thankful

1. I, _____, am_____ for_____,

    because_____

2. I, _____, am_____ for_____,

    because_____

I am Fit

1. I, _____, am_____

because_____

2. I, _____, am_____

because_____

Most important tasks of the day?

1._____

2._____

I ate this enhancing super whole food

☐ Carrots ☐ Lentils ☐ Cabbage ☐ Other_____

Nutrition

The daily recommend intake of magnesium for an adult male is?
☐ 15 mg ☐ 35 mg ☐ 100 mg ☐ 400 mg

Magnesium is a co-factor for over 100 enzymes involved in blood sugar control? TRUE OR FALSE? _____

Magnesium supplementation (300mg) is scientifically proven to heal some forms of major depression? TRUE OR FALSE? _____

Have you eaten a food with abundant magnesium this week?

☐ Spinach ☐ Beet Greens ☐ Pumpkin Seeds ☐ Swiss Chard

I Acknowledge

Three fantastic things that happened today?

1. _____

2. _____

3. _____

I laughed or smiled today because

_____

How will I enhance tomorrow?

_____

"You are what you repeatedly do. Excellence is not an event - it is a habit."
- Aristotle

Laughter Day!

Pretend to laugh for 10 seconds!

Visualize a family member or close friend Smiling and Laughing

Visualize a colleague Smiling and Laughing

Visualize someone you don't know Smiling and Laughing

Pretend to laugh for 10 seconds

Thank you, Universe, for?

<u>NOTES</u>

Pretend to Laugh for 10 seconds :)!!!

I am Thankful

1. I, _____, am_____ for_____,

   because_____

2. I, _____, am_____ for_____,

   because_____

I am Gorgeous

1. I, _____, am_____

because_____

2. I, _____, am_____

because_____

Most important tasks of the day?

1._____

2._____

I ate this enhancing super whole food

☐ Pumpkin Seeds ☐ Lentils ☐ Cabbage ☐ Other_____

Nutrition

The daily recommend intake of Folate for an adult male is?
☐ 15 mcg ☐ 35 mcg ☐ 100 mcg ☐ 400 mcg

Folate is needed to produce dopamine and serotonin? TRUE OR FALSE? _____

Folic acid supplementation (400mcg) is scientifically proven to reduce proinflammatory cytokines? TRUE OR FALSE? _____

Have you eaten a food with abundant folate this week?

☐ Lentils ☐ Spinach ☐ Asparagus ☐ Beets

I Acknowledge

Three fantastic things that happened today?

1._____

2._____

3._____

I laughed or smiled today because

_____

How will I enhance tomorrow?

_____

"The ultimate measure of a man is not where he stands in moments of comfort and convenience, but where he stands at times of challenge and controversy."
- Dr. Martin Luther King, Jr.

Pretend to Laugh for 10 seconds :)!!!

I am Thankful

1. I, _____, am_____ for_____,

   because_____

2. I, _____, am_____ for_____,

   because_____

I am Smart

1. I, _____, am_____

because_____

2. I, _____, am_____

because_____

Most important tasks of the day?

1._____

2._____

I ate this enhancing super whole food
☐ Pumpkin Seeds ☐Lentils ☐ Beets ☐Other_____

Nutrition

The daily recommend intake of Iodine is?
☐ 15 mcg ☐ 35 mcg ☐ 100 mcg ☐ 150 mcg

Iodine is needed to produce thyroid hormone? TRUE OR FALSE?
_____

Have you eaten a food with abundant iodine this week?

☐ Sea Vegetables ☐ Cod ☐ Shrimp ☐ Scallops

I Acknowledge

Three fantastic things that happened today?
1._____

2._____

3._____

I laughed or smiled today because

_____

How will I enhance tomorrow?

_____

"Things that matter most must never be at the mercy of things that matter least."
- Johann Wolfgang von Goethe

Pretend to Laugh for 10 seconds :)!!!

I am Thankful

1.   I, _____, am_____ for_____,

    because_____

2.   I, _____, am_____ for_____,

    because_____

I am Passionate

1.   I, _____, am_____

because_____

2.   I, _____, am_____

because_____

Most important tasks of the day?

1._____

2._____

I ate this enhancing super whole food
☐ Pumpkin Seeds ☐ Lentils ☐ Apple ☐ Other_____

Nutrition

The daily recommend intake of selenium for an adult is?
☐ 5 mcg ☐ 35 mcg ☐ 40 mcg ☐ 55 mcg

Selenium is needed to produce the detoxifying enzyme glutathione peroxidase? TRUE OR FALSE? _____

Selenium supplementation (5mcg/kg/bw) is scientifically proven to reduce fluoride poisoning? TRUE OR FALSE? _____

Have you eaten a food with abundant selenium this week?

☐ Tuna ☐ Shrimp ☐ Salmon ☐ Cod

I Acknowledge

Three fantastic things that happened today?

1._____

2._____

3._____

I laughed or smiled today because

_____

How will I enhance tomorrow?

_____

**"If you realized how powerful your thoughts are,
you would never think another negative thought." - Peace Pilgrim**

Pretend to Laugh for 10 seconds :)!!!

I am Thankful

1.   I, _____, am_____ for_____,

    because_____

2.   I, _____, am_____ for_____,

    because_____

I am Loved

1.   I, _____, am_____

because_____

2.   I, _____, am_____

because_____

Most important tasks of the day?

    1._____

    2._____

I ate this enhancing super whole food

☐ Pumpkin Seeds ☐ Lentils ☐ Cabbage ☐ Other_____

Relaxation

Acupuncture and massage are proven to induce weight-loss? TRUE OR FALSE? _____

Breathing through your nose can increase cognitive function? TRUE OR FALSE? _____

I Acknowledge

Three fantastic things that happened today?

1._____

2._____

3._____

I laughed or smiled today because

_____

How will I enhance tomorrow?

_____

"There are essentially two things that will make us wiser: the books we read and the people we meet." -Charles Jones

<u>Laughter Day!</u>

Pretend to laugh for 10 seconds!

Visualize a family member or close friend Smiling and Laughing

Visualize a colleague Smiling and Laughing

Visualize someone you don't know Smiling and Laughing

Pretend to laugh for 10 seconds

Thank you, Universe, for?

NOTES

Pretend to Laugh for 10 seconds :)!!!

I am Thankful

1.   I, _____, am_____ for_____,

    because_____

2.   I, _____, am_____ for_____,

    because_____

I am Spectacular

1.   I, _____, am_____

because_____

2.   I, _____, am_____

because_____

Most important tasks of the day?

1._____

2._____

I ate this enhancing super whole food
☐ Fish ☐Lentils ☐ Almonds ☐Other_____

Aluminum

Aluminum causes Alzheimer's like symptoms in mice?
TRUE OR FALSE? _____

Aluminum from aluminum adjuvant used in vaccines is proven to damage the brain? TRUE OR FALSE_____?

Aluminum is widely recognized as a neurotoxin? TRUE OR FALSE?
_____

Spirulina is proven to detoxify aluminum? TRUE OR FALSE? _____

I Acknowledge

Three fantastic things that happened today?

1._____

2._____

3._____

I laughed or smiled today because

_____

How will I enhance tomorrow?

_____

"The average person puts about 25% of his energy and ability into his work. The world takes its hat off to those who put more than 50% of their capacity into their work, and the world stands on its head for those few and far between who devote 100%."
- Andrew Carnegie

Pretend to Laugh for 10 seconds :)!!!

I am Thankful

1. I, _____, am_____ for_____,

    because_____

2. I, _____, am_____ for_____,

    because_____

I am Fit

1. I, _____, am_____

because_____

2. I, _____, am_____

because_____

Most important tasks of the day?

1._____

2._____

I ate this enhancing super whole food
☐ Beets ☐ Lentils ☐ Cabbage ☐ Other_____

Fluoride

Fluoride is neurotoxic? TRUE OR FALSE? _____

According to fluoride toothpaste labels, toothpaste should not be swallowed? TRUE OR FALSE? _____

Curcumin supplementation (30mg/kg/bw) is scientifically proven to reduce fluoride-based brain damage? TRUE OR FALSE? _____

I Acknowledge

Three fantastic things that happened today?

1._____

2._____

3._____

I laughed or smiled today because

_____

How will I enhance tomorrow?

_____

"Nothing great was ever achieved without enthusiasm."
- Ralph Waldo Emerson

Pretend to Laugh for 10 seconds :)!!!

I am Thankful

1. I, _____, am_____ for_____,

because_____

2. I, _____, am_____ for_____,

because_____

I am Impressive

1. I, _____, am_____

because_____

2. I, _____, am_____

because_____

Most important tasks of the day?

1._____

2._____

I ate this enhancing super whole food
☐ Spirulina ☐ Lentils ☐ Cabbage ☐ Other_____

Nutrition

Zinc (30 mg) increases testosterone? TRUE OR FALSE?
_____

Zinc supplementation (1mg/kg/bw) is scientifically proven to reduce lead levels in mammalian bodies? TRUE OR FALSE? _____

Have you eaten a food with abundant zinc this week?

☐ Spinach ☐ Sesame Seeds ☐ Asparagus ☐ Pumpkin Seeds

I Acknowledge

Three fantastic things that happened today?

1._____

2._____

3._____

I laughed or smiled today because

_____

How will I enhance tomorrow?

_____

"To accomplish great things, we must not only act, but also dream, not only plan, but also believe." - Anatole France

Pretend to Laugh for 10 seconds :)!!!

I am Thankful

1.   I, _____, am_____ for_____,

      because_____

2.   I, _____, am_____ for_____,

      because_____

I am a Remarkable Listener

1.   I, _____, am_____

because_____

2.   I, _____, am_____

because_____

Most important tasks of the day?

      1._____

      2._____

I ate this enhancing super whole food
☐ Pumpkin Seeds ☐ Lentils ☐ Celery ☐ Other_____

Nutrition

Vitamin K is essential for blood clotting and bone health?
TRUE OR FALSE? _____

Vitamin K supplementation is scientifically proven to reduce bone fractures?
TRUE OR FALSE? _____

Have you eaten a food with abundant vitamin k this week?

☐ Kale　☐ Spinach　☐ Collard Greens　☐ Beet Greens

I Acknowledge

Three fantastic things that happened today?

1._____

2._____

3._____

I laughed or smiled today because

_____

How will I enhance tomorrow?

_____

**"I am a great believer in luck, and I find that the harder I work
the more luck I have."**
- Thomas Jefferson

<u>Laughter Day!</u>

Pretend to laugh for 10 seconds!

Visualize a family member or close friend Smiling and Laughing

Visualize a colleague Smiling and Laughing

Visualize someone you don't know Smiling and Laughing

Pretend to laugh for 10 seconds

Thank you, Universe, for?

NOTES

Pretend to Laugh for 10 seconds :)!!!

I am Thankful

1.   I, _____, am_____ for_____,
   because_____

2.   I, _____, am_____ for_____,
   because_____

I am Hot

1.   I, _____, am_____
because_____

2.   I, _____, am_____
because_____

Most important tasks of the day?

1._____

2._____

I ate this enhancing super whole food
☐ Potato ☐ Lentils ☐ Cabbage ☐ Other_____

Pesticide

Rotenone a pesticide used on organic and conventional produce is used to induce Parkinson's in mice? TRUE OR FALSE?

_____

Sulforaphane supplementation is proven to protect against rotenone neurotoxicity? TRUE OR FALSE? _____

Have you eaten a food with abundant sulforaphane this week?

☐ Broccoli Sprouts ☐ Spinach ☐ Broccoli ☐ Kale

I Acknowledge

Three fantastic things that happened today?

1._____

2._____

3._____

I laughed or smiled today because

_____

How will I enhance tomorrow?

_____

"If you want your life to be a magnificent story, then begin by realizing that you are the author and every day you have the opportunity to write a new page." - Mark Houlahan

Pretend to Laugh for 10 seconds :)!!!

I am Thankful

1.   I, _____ , am_____ for_____ ,
     because_____

2.   I, _____ , am_____ for_____ ,
     because_____

I am inspired

1.   I, _____ , am_____
because_____

2.   I, _____ , am_____
because_____

Most important tasks of the day?

1._____

2._____

I ate this enhancing super whole food

☐ Apple ☐Broccoli Sprouts ☐ Cabbage ☐Other_____

Processed Food toxins

Alloxan causes diabetes in mice and is a byproduct of bleached flour?
TRUE OR FALSE? _____

MSG consumption causes mice to become fat?
TRUE OR FALSE? _____

Heating carbs at very high temperatures produces the carcinogen acrylamide? TRUE OR FALSE? _____

Have you eaten a food that contains acrylamide this week?

☐ Fries ☐ Chips ☐ KFC ☐ Pizza

I Acknowledge

Three fantastic things that happened today?

1._____

2._____

3._____

I laughed or smiled today because

_____

How will I enhance tomorrow?

_____

"I do believe I am special. My special gift is my vision, my commitment, and my willingness to do whatever it takes."
- Anthony Robbins

Pretend to Laugh for 10 seconds :)!!!

I am Thankful

1. I, _____, am_____ for_____,

    because_____

2. I, _____, am_____ for_____,

    because_____

I am Wealthy

1. I, _____, am_____

because_____

2. I, _____, am_____

because_____

Most important tasks of the day?

1._____

2._____

I ate this enhancing super whole food

☐ Blueberries ☐ Lentils ☐ Avocado ☐ Other_____

Natural toxins

Boiling can reduce deadly lecithin and phytates contained naturally in beans. by?

☐ 0% ☐ 5% ☐ 10% ☐ Over 90%

Fumonisin a natural toxin in corn causes pellagra?

TRUE OR FALSE? _____

Fumonisin can be reduced via lime and alkalization?
TRUE OR FALSE? _____

I Acknowledge

Three fantastic things that happened today?

1._____

2._____

3._____

I laughed or smiled today because

_____

How will I enhance tomorrow?

_____

"It's not whether you get knocked down; it's whether you get back up."
- Vince Lombardi

Pretend to Laugh for 10 seconds :)!!!

I am Thankful

1.   I, _____, am_____ for_____,

   because_____

2.   I, _____, am_____ for_____,

   because_____

I am Aroused

1.   I, _____, am_____

because_____

2.   I, _____, am_____

because_____

Most important tasks of the day?

   1._____

   2._____

I ate this enhancing super whole food

☐ Onion ☐ Lemon ☐ Cabbage ☐ Other_____

Nutrition

Bisphenol A (BPA) is classified as an obesogene?
TRUE OR FALSE? _____

Frozen food contains less BPA than canned food?
TRUE OR FALSE? _____

BPA or BPA like chemicals are sprayed on all cans to prevent erosion?
TRUE OR FALSE? _____

Frozen food contains 70% less pesticides?
TRUE OR FALSE? _____

I Acknowledge

Three fantastic things that happened today?

1._____

2._____

3._____

I laughed or smiled today because

_____

How will I enhance tomorrow?

_____

"Anyone who has never made a mistake has never tried anything new."
- Albert Einstien

<u>Laughter Day!</u>

Pretend to laugh for 10 seconds!

Visualize a family member or close friend Smiling and Laughing

Visualize a colleague Smiling and Laughing

Visualize someone you don't know Smiling and Laughing

Pretend to laugh for 10 seconds

Thank you, Universe, for?

NOTES

Pretend to Laugh for 10 seconds :)!!!

I am Thankful

1.   I, _____, am_____ for_____,

   because_____

2.   I, _____, am_____ for_____,

   because_____

I am In Love

1.   I, _____, am_____

because_____

2.   I, _____, am_____

because_____

Most important tasks of the day?

1._____

2._____

I ate this enhancing super whole food

☐ Mussels ☐ Garlic ☐ Cabbage ☐ Other_____

Inflammation

Taking vitamins and minerals can reduce inflammation?
TRUE OR FALSE? _____

WI-FI induces inflammation and inhibits healing?
TRUE OR FALSE? _____

Depressed, schizophrenic and autistic people are extremely inflamed with cytokines? TRUE OR FALSE? _____

I Acknowledge

Three fantastic things that happened today?

1._____

2._____

3._____

I laughed or smiled today because

_____

How will I enhance tomorrow?

_____

"Some men give up their designs when they have almost reached their goal, while others obtain a victory by exerting, at the last moment, more vigorous efforts than ever before." - Herodotus

Pretend to Laugh for 10 seconds :)!!!

I am Thankful

1. I, _____, am_____ for_____,

    because_____

2. I, _____, am_____ for_____,

    because_____

I am Gorgeous

1. I, _____, am_____

because_____

2. I, _____, am_____

because_____

Most important tasks of the day?

1._____

2._____

I ate this enhancing super whole food

☐ Green Onion ☐ Parsley ☐ Cabbage ☐ Other_____

Water

In general, spring water contains less toxins like lead than city water?
TRUE OR FALSE? _____

Water filters can be used to reduce toxins?
TRUE OR FALSE? _____

Cities test their waters for a very limited number of toxins and BPA is not one of them? TRUE OR FALSE? _____

I Acknowledge

Three fantastic things that happened today?

1. _____

2. _____

3. _____

I laughed or smiled today because

_____

How will I enhance tomorrow?

_____

"To me, a winner is someone who recognizes their God-given talents,
works his tail off to develop them into skills,
and uses those skills to accomplish his goals.
Even when I lost, I learned what my weaknesses were,
and I went out the next day to turn those weaknesses into strengths."
-Larry Bird

Pretend to Laugh for 10 seconds :)!!!

I am Thankful

1.   I, _____, am _____ for _____,

    because _____

2.   I, _____, am _____ for _____,

    because _____

I am Leader

1.   I, _____, am _____

because _____

2.   I, _____, am _____

because _____

Most important tasks of the day?

1. _____

2. _____

I ate this enhancing super whole food

☐ Pineapple ☐ Red Onion ☐ Cabbage ☐ Other _____

Nutrition

The daily recommend intake of Choline for an adult male is?
☐ 15 mg ☐ 35 mg ☐ 100 mg ☐ 400 mg

Choline is needed for learning? TRUE OR FALSE? _____

Choline supplementation (800mg) is scientifically proven to increase cognitive performance? TRUE OR FALSE? _____

Have you eaten a food with abundant choline this week?

☐ Shrimp ☐ Eggs ☐ Scallops ☐ Cod

I Acknowledge

Three fantastic things that happened today?

1._____

2._____

3._____

I laughed or smiled today because

_____

How will I enhance tomorrow?

_____

"To be a champion, you have to believe in yourself when nobody else will."
- Sugar Ray Robinson

<u>Laughter Day!</u>

Pretend to laugh for 10 seconds!

Visualize a family member or close friend Smiling and Laughing

Visualize a colleague Smiling and Laughing

Visualize someone you don't know Smiling and Laughing

Pretend to laugh for 10 seconds

Thank you, Universe, for?

NOTES

Pretend to Laugh for 10 seconds :)!!!

I am Thankful

1. I, _____ , am_____ for_____ ,

   because_____

2. I, _____ , am_____ for_____ ,

   because_____

I am Breathing

1. I, _____ , am_____

because_____

2. I, _____ , am_____

because_____

Most important tasks of the day?

1._____

2._____

I ate this enhancing super whole food

☐ Pumpkin Seeds ☐ Carrots ☐ Peas ☐ Other_____

Nutrition

Tea contains caffeine? TRUE OR FALSE? _____

Sugar increases dopamine like cocaine?
TRUE OR FALSE? _____

Sugar induces non-alcoholic fatty liver disease? TRUE OR FALSE?
_____

Consuming 75 g of sugar reduces testosterone by?

☐ **0%** ☐ **5%** ☐ **10%** ☐ **25%**

I Acknowledge

Three fantastic things that happened today?

1._____

2._____

3._____

I laughed or smiled today because

_____

How will I enhance tomorrow?

_____

"Your ideas are like diamonds...without the refining process, they are just a dirty rock, but by cutting away the impurities, they become priceless."
- Paul Kearly

Pretend to Laugh for 10 seconds :)!!!

I am Thankful

1.   I, _____, am_____ for_____,

   because_____

2.   I, _____, am_____ for_____,

   because_____

I am a Champion

1.   I, _____, am_____

because_____

2.   I, _____, am_____

because_____

Most important tasks of the day?

1._____

2._____

I ate this enhancing super whole food

☐ Kale ☐ Spinach ☐ Cabbage ☐ Other_____

Non-Stick

Non-stick (PTFE) cookware when heated at high temperatures, releases extremely deadly gases like perfluoropropene? TRUE OR FALSE? _____

Stainless steel pans and pots are great way to avoid PTFE derived gases? TRUE OR FALSE? _____

I Acknowledge

Three fantastic things that happened today?

1._____

2._____

3._____

I laughed or smiled today because

_____

How will I enhance tomorrow?

_____

"Winning is not a "sometime" thing. You don't win once in a while, you don't do things right once in a while, you do them right all of the time. Winning is a habit, unfortunately, so is losing." --Vince Lomardi

Pretend to Laugh for 10 seconds :)!!!

I am Thankful

1.   I, _____, am_____ for_____,

    because_____

2.   I, _____, am_____ for_____,

    because_____

I am Smart

1.   I, _____, am_____

because_____

2.   I, _____, am_____

because_____

Most important tasks of the day?

   1._____

   2._____

I ate this enhancing super whole food

☐ Mustard Seeds ☐ Coriander ☐ Garlic ☐ Other_____

Nutrition

Garlic contains anti-inflammatory phytochemical called allicin?
TRUE OR FALSE? _____

Turmeric contains curcumin? TRUE OR FALSE? _____

Curcumin supplementation (400 mg) is scientifically proven to improve working memory and mood?
TRUE OR FALSE? _____

I Acknowledge

Three fantastic things that happened today?

1._____

2._____

3._____

I laughed or smiled today because

_____

How will I enhance tomorrow?

_____

"People become successful the minute they decide to."
- Harvey Mackay

Pretend to Laugh for 10 seconds :)!!!

I am Thankful

1.   I, _____, am_____ for_____,

because_____

2.   I, _____, am_____ for_____,

because_____

I am Strong

1.   I, _____, am_____

because_____

2.   I, _____, am_____

because_____

Most important tasks of the day?

1._____

2._____

I ate this enhancing super whole food

☐ Kale ☐ Kidney Beans ☐ Mushrooms ☐ Other_____

Toxins

**TALC powder in baby powder causes cancer?
TRUE OR FALSE?** _____

**Bromine is toxic and found in most cars?
TRUE OR FALSE?** _____

Household cleaners contain volatile organic compounds that contaminate your air? TRUE OR FALSE? _____

I Acknowledge

Three fantastic things that happened today?

1._____

2._____

3._____

I laughed or smiled today because

_____

How will I enhance tomorrow?

_____

**"The greatest discovery of all time is that a person can change his future by merely changing his attitude."
-Oprah Winfrey**

<u>Laughter Day!</u>

Pretend to laugh for 10 seconds!

Visualize a family member or close friend Smiling and Laughing

Visualize a colleague Smiling and Laughing

Visualize someone you don't know Smiling and Laughing

Pretend to laugh for 10 seconds

Thank you, Universe, for?

NOTES

Pretend to Laugh for 10 seconds :)!!!

I am Thankful

1.　I, _____, am_____ for_____,

　　because_____

2.　I, _____, am_____ for_____,

　　because_____

I am Loved

1.　I, _____, am_____

because_____

2.　I, _____, am_____

because_____

Most important tasks of the day?

　　1._____

　　2._____

I ate this enhancing super whole food

☐ Quinoa ☐ Lentils ☐ Brown Rice ☐ Other_____

Nutrition

Mega doses of vitamins and minerals have dramatically improved the mental abilities of some mentally handicap kids?
TRUE OR FALSE? _____

Niacin greatly improves symptoms of schizophrenia?
TRUE OR FALSE? _____

Vitamin C is essential for beautiful skin and strong bones?
TRUE OR FALSE? _____

Have you eaten a food with abundant vitamin C this week?

☐ **Bell Pepper** ☐ **Broccoli** ☐ **Pineapple** ☐ **Brussels Sprouts**

I Acknowledge

Three fantastic things that happened today?

1._____

2._____

3._____

I laughed or smiled today because

_____

How will I enhance tomorrow?

_____

"If you cannot do great things, then do small things in a great way."
-Napoleon Hill

Pretend to Laugh for 10 seconds :)!!!

I am Thankful

1. I, _____, am_____ for_____,

   because_____

2. I, _____, am_____ for_____,

   because_____

I am Excited

1. I, _____, am_____

because_____

2. I, _____, am_____

because_____

Most important tasks of the day?

1._____

2._____

I ate this enhancing super whole food

☐ Apple ☐ Lentils ☐ Cabbage ☐ Other_____

Nutrition

Minerals work optimally in a precise range of ratios?
TRUE OR FALSE? _____

There are 8 different types of vitamin E?
TRUE OR FALSE? _____

Supplementing calcium without phosphorous and magnesium can be harmful? TRUE OR FALSE? _____

I Acknowledge

Three fantastic things that happened today?

1._____

2._____

3._____

I laughed or smiled today because

_____

How will I enhance tomorrow?

_____

"Those who dare to fail miserably can achieve greatly."
-John F. Kennedy

Pretend to Laugh for 10 seconds :)!!!

I am Thankful

1. I, _____ , am_____ for_____ ,

    because_____

2. I, _____ , am_____ for_____ ,

    because_____

I am Funny

1. I, _____ , am_____

because_____

2. I, _____ , am_____

because_____

Most important tasks of the day?

1._____

2._____

I ate this enhancing super whole food

☐Fermented Veggies ☐ Cabbage ☐Other_____

Nutrition

Fermented Foods contain life-enhancing bacteria?
TRUE OR FALSE? _____

Fermentation, sprouting, soaking, germinating can greatly reduce gluten? TRUE OR FALSE? _____

Corn, rice and wheat contain gluten?
TRUE OR FALSE? _____

I Acknowledge

Three fantastic things that happened today?

1._____

2._____

3._____

I laughed or smiled today because

_____

How will I enhance tomorrow?

_____

"I like to listen. I have learned a great deal from listening carefully.
Most people never listen."
–Ernest Hemingway

Pretend to Laugh for 10 seconds :)!!!

I am Thankful

1.   I, _____, am_____ for_____,

    because_____

2.   I, _____, am_____ for_____,

    because_____

I am Encouraging

1.   I, _____, am_____

because_____

2.   I, _____, am_____

because_____

Most important tasks of the day?

1._____

2._____

I ate this enhancing super whole food

☐ Pumpkin Seeds ☐Cod ☐ Salmon ☐Other_____

Nutrition

Chlorella detoxifies dioxins? TRUE OR FALSE? _____

**DHA is the most abundant fat in the brain?
TRUE OR FALSE?** _____

**DHA is mostly found in sea food?
TRUE OR FALSE?** _____

I Acknowledge

Three fantastic things that happened today?

1._____

2._____

3._____

I laughed or smiled today because

_____

How will I enhance tomorrow?

_____

**"Choose a job you love, and you will never have to work a day in your life."
-Confucious**

Laughter Day!

Pretend to laugh for 10 seconds!

Visualize a family member or close friend Smiling and Laughing

Visualize a colleague Smiling and Laughing

Visualize someone you don't know Smiling and Laughing

Pretend to laugh for 10 seconds

Thank you, Universe, for?

NOTES

Pretend to Laugh for 10 seconds :)!!!

I am Thankful

1. I, _____, am_____ for_____,

   because_____

2. I, _____, am_____ for_____,

   because_____

I am Happy

1. I, _____, am_____

because_____

2. I, _____, am_____

because_____

Most important tasks of the day?

1._____

2._____

I ate this enhancing super whole food

☐ Eggs ☐ Fish ☐ Coconut Oil ☐ Other_____

Nutrition

Every vegetable and fruit contains unique life-enhancing phytochemicals?
TRUE OR FALSE? _____

Consuming beets can increase your brain blood flow?
TRUE OR FALSE? _____

Consuming carbonated water can increase your brain blood flow?
TRUE OR FALSE? _____

I Acknowledge

Three fantastic things that happened today?

1._____

2._____

3._____

I laughed or smiled today because

_____

How will I enhance tomorrow?

_____

"Do not wait; the time will never be 'just right'. Start where you stand, and work with whatever tools you may have at your command, and better tools will be found as you go along."
-George Herbert

Pretend to Laugh for 10 seconds :)!!!

I am Thankful

1. I, _____, am_____ for_____,

    because_____

2. I, _____, am_____ for_____,

    because_____

I am Muscular

1. I, _____, am_____

because_____

2. I, _____, am_____

because_____

Most important tasks of the day?

1._____

2._____

I ate this enhancing super whole food

☐ Eggs ☐Fish ☐ Olive Oil ☐Other_____

Nutrition

In your gut, there are vitamin-producing and toxin-eliminating bacteria that depend on fiber to survive? TRUE OR FALSE?

_____

Lactobacillus brevis DPC6108 converts dangerous MSG into relaxing GABA?
TRUE OR FALSE? _____

Prebiotics are non-digestible food ingredients that promote the growth of beneficial microorganisms in the intestines like fiber and resistant starch?
TRUE or FALSE_____?

I Acknowledge

Three fantastic things that happened today?

1._____

2._____

3._____

I laughed or smiled today because

_____

How will I enhance tomorrow?

_____

"Strength does not come from winning. Your struggles develop your strengths. When you go through hardships and decide not to surrender, that is strength."
—Arnold Schwarzenegger

Pretend to Laugh for 10 seconds :)!!!

I am Thankful

1. I, _____, am_____ for_____,

    because_____

2. I, _____, am_____ for_____,

    because_____

I am Rich

1. I, _____, am_____

because_____

2. I, _____, am_____

because_____

Most important tasks of the day?

1._____

2._____

I ate this enhancing super whole food

☐ Eggs ☐ Fish ☐ Coriander ☐ Other_____

Nutrition

The dry weight of the Brain is made of 60% fat. Put INTO YOUR OWN WORDS OR RECOPY _____

Chewing gum can increase concentration and mathematical ability. Put INTO YOUR OWN WORDS OR
RECOPY_____

I Acknowledge

Three fantastic things that happened today?

1._____

2._____

3._____

I laughed or smiled today because

_____

How will I enhance tomorrow?

_____

"Your time is limited, don't waste it living someone else's life. Don't be trapped by dogma, which is living the result of other people's thinking. Don't let the noise of other opinions drown your own inner voice. And most important, have the courage to follow your heart and intuition, they somehow already know what you truly want to become. Everything else is secondary."
Steve Jobs

Pretend to Laugh for 10 seconds :)!!!

I am Thankful

1.   I, _____, am_____ for_____,

   because_____

2.   I, _____, am_____ for_____,

   because_____

I am Dazzling

1.   I, _____, am_____

because_____

2.   I, _____, am_____

because_____

Most important tasks of the day?

1._____

2._____

I ate this enhancing super whole food

☐ Eggs ☐ Fish ☐ Oatmeal ☐ Other_____

Nutrition

Essential oils can be infused in the air to heal people. Put INTO YOUR OWN WORDS OR
RECOPY_____

Niels Ryberg Finsen won the Nobel Prize in Medicine in 1903 for healing small pox with red light. Put INTO YOUR OWN WORDS OR
RECOPY_____

I Acknowledge

Three fantastic things that happened today?
1._____

2._____

3._____

I laughed or smiled today because

_____

How will I enhance tomorrow?

_____

"There are better starters than me but I'm a strong finisher." — Usain Bolt

Laughter Day!

Pretend to laugh for 10 seconds!

Visualize a family member or close friend Smiling and Laughing

Visualize a colleague Smiling and Laughing

Visualize someone you don't know Smiling and Laughing

Pretend to laugh for 10 seconds

Thank you, Universe, for?

NOTES

Pretend to Laugh for 10 seconds :)!!!

I am Thankful

1.   I, _____, am_____ for_____,

because_____

2.   I, _____, am_____ for_____,

because_____

I am Ecstatic

1.   I, _____, am_____

because_____

2.   I, _____, am_____

because_____

Most important tasks of the day?

1._____

2._____

I ate this enhancing super whole food

☐ Eggs ☐Fish ☐ Germinated beans ☐Other_____

Nutrition

Over $190 million has been award to victims of Johnson & Johnson's baby powder because the baby powder caused them ovarian cancer. PUT INTO YOUR OWN WORDS OR
RECOPY_____

I Acknowledge

Three fantastic things that happened today?

1._____

2._____

3._____

I laughed or smiled today because

_____

How will I enhance tomorrow?

_____

"All the adversity I've had in my life, all my troubles and obstacles, have strengthened me.... You may not realize it when it happens, but a kick in the teeth may be the best thing in the world for you."
—Walt Disney

Pretend to Laugh for 10 seconds :)!!!

I am Thankful

1.   I, _____, am_____ for_____,

because_____

2.   I, _____, am_____ for_____,

because_____

I am Happy

1.   I, _____, am_____

because_____

2.   I, _____, am_____

because_____

Most important tasks of the day?

1._____

2._____

I ate this enhancing super whole food

☐ Eggs ☐ Fish ☐ Carrots ☐ Other_____

Nutrition

Soaking foods into baking soda is proven to remove pesticides. PUT INTO YOUR OWN WORDS OR
RECOPY_____

Baking soda is used as a treatment for metabolic acidosis in hospitals. PUT INTO YOUR OWN WORDS OR
RECOPY_____

I Acknowledge

Three fantastic things that happened today?

1._____

2._____

3._____

I laughed or smiled today because

_____

How will I enhance tomorrow?

_____

"A truly strong person does not need the approval of others any more than a lion needs the approval of sheep."
—Vernon Howard

Pretend to Laugh for 10 seconds :)!!!

I am Thankful

1. I, _____, am_____ for_____,

    because_____

2. I, _____, am_____ for_____,

    because_____

I am Smiling

1. I, _____, am_____

because_____

2. I, _____, am_____

because_____

Most important tasks of the day?

1._____

2._____

I ate this enhancing super whole food

☐ Eggs ☐Fish ☐ Apples ☐Other_____

Nutrition

Most studies funded by the wireless communication industry conclude that EMF radiation has no effect. PUT INTO YOUR OWN WORDS OR RECOPY_____

Most non-industry funded studies conclude that EMF radiation has negative effects. PUT INTO YOUR OWN WORDS OR RECOPY_____

I Acknowledge

Three fantastic things that happened today?

1._____

2._____

3._____

I laughed or smiled today because

_____

How will I enhance tomorrow?

_____

"Strength and growth come only through continuous effort and struggle." —Napoleon Hill

Pretend to Laugh for 10 seconds :)!!!

I am Thankful

1.   I, _____ , am_____ for_____ ,

because_____

2.   I, _____ , am_____ for_____ ,

because_____

I am Singing

1.   I, _____ , am_____

because_____

2.   I, _____ , am_____

because_____

Most important tasks of the day?

1._____

2._____

I ate this enhancing super whole food

☐ Eggs ☐ Fish ☐ Olives ☐ Other_____

Nutrition

Avocado and coconut oil have higher smoking points than olive oil.
PUT INTO YOUR OWN WORDS OR
RECOPY_____

I Acknowledge

Three fantastic things that happened today?

1._____

2._____

3._____

I laughed or smiled today because

_____

How will I enhance tomorrow?

_____

"Make up your mind that no matter what comes your way, no matter how difficult, no matter how unfair, you will do more than simply survive. You will thrive in spite of it." —Joel Osteen

Pretend to Laugh for 10 seconds :)!!!

I am Thankful

1. I, _____, am_____ for_____,

   because_____

2. I, _____, am_____ for_____,

   because_____

I am Knowledgeable

1. I, _____, am_____

because_____

2. I, _____, am_____

because_____

Most important tasks of the day?

1._____

2._____

I ate this enhancing super whole food

☐ Eggs ☐ Fish ☐ Nuts ☐ Other_____

Nutrition

Milk contains phthalates because milk is drawn through plastic tubes. PUT INTO YOUR OWN WORDS OR
RECOPY_____

Pasteurized milk is stripped of crucial enzymes like catalase that help digest milk. PUT INTO YOUR OWN WORDS OR
RECOPY_____

I Acknowledge

Three fantastic things that happened today?

1._____

2._____

3._____

I laughed or smiled today because

_____

How will I enhance tomorrow?

_____

"You must learn from the mistakes of others. You can't possibly live long enough to make them all yourself."
- Sam Levenson

Laughter Day!

Pretend to laugh for 10 seconds!

Visualize a family member or close friend Smiling and Laughing

Visualize a colleague Smiling and Laughing

Visualize someone you don't know Smiling and Laughing

Pretend to laugh for 10 seconds

Thank you, Universe, for?

NOTES

Pretend to Laugh for 10 seconds :)!!!

I am Thankful

1. I, _____, am_____ for_____,

   because_____

2. I, _____, am_____ for_____,

   because_____

I am Brilliant

1. I, _____, am_____

because_____

2. I, _____, am_____

because_____

Most important tasks of the day?

1._____

2._____

I ate this enhancing super whole food

☐ Eggs ☐ Fish ☐ Cucumber ☐ Other_____

Nutrition

Plants can release oxygen and remove toxins from the air. PUT INTO YOUR OWN WORDS OR RECOPY _____

I Acknowledge

Three fantastic things that happened today?

1._____

2._____

3._____

I laughed or smiled today because

_____

How will I enhance tomorrow?

_____

"The biggest sin is sitting on your ass."
- Florynce Kennedy

Pretend to Laugh for 10 seconds :)!!!

I am Thankful

1. I, _____, am_____ for_____,

   because_____

2. I, _____, am_____ for_____,

   because_____

I am Sexy

1. I, _____, am_____

because_____

2. I, _____, am_____

because_____

Most important tasks of the day?

1._____

2._____

I ate this enhancing super whole food

☐ Eggs ☐ Fish ☐ Almonds ☐ Other_____

Nutrition

Jimmy Gonzalez, an attorney, died from brain cancer that was caused by the radiation emitted from his mobile phone. PUT INTO YOUR OWN WORDS OR RECOPY_____

180-day fermented miso is proven to reduce effects of radiation. Put INTO YOUR OWN WORDS OR RECOPY_____

I Acknowledge

Three fantastic things that happened today?

1._____

2._____

3._____

I laughed or smiled today because

_____

How will I enhance tomorrow?

_____

"I find television very educational. Every time someone turns it on, I go in the other room and read a book."
– Groucho Marx

Pretend to Laugh for 10 seconds :)!!!

I am Thankful

1. I, _____, am_____ for_____,

    because_____

2. I, _____, am_____ for_____,

    because_____

I am Strong

1. I, _____, am_____

because_____

2. I, _____, am_____

because_____

Most important tasks of the day?

1._____

2._____

I ate this enhancing super whole food

☐ Eggs ☐ Fish ☐ Kale ☐ Other_____

Nutrition

A chemical in Windex called Sodium dodecylbenzene sulfonate, is more lethal than lead. PUT INTO YOUR OWN WORDS OR
RECOPY_____

I Acknowledge

Three fantastic things that happened today?

1._____

2._____

3._____

I laughed or smiled today because

_____

How will I enhance tomorrow?

_____

"Opportunity does not knock, it presents itself when you beat down the door." – Kyle Chandler

Pretend to Laugh for 10 seconds :)!!!

I am Thankful

1. I, _____, am_____ for_____,

   because_____

2. I, _____, am_____ for_____,

   because_____

I am Passionate

1. I, _____, am_____

becuase_____

2. I, _____, am_____

because_____

Most important tasks of the day?

1._____

2._____

I ate this enhancing super whole food

☐ Eggs ☐ Fish ☐ Spinach ☐ Other_____

Nutrition

MSG is only included in a product's ingredient list if the product contains 99%-to-100% MSG. PUT INTO YOUR OWN WORDS OR RECOPY_____

I Acknowledge

Three fantastic things that happened today?

1._____

2._____

3._____

I laughed or smiled today because

_____

How will I enhance tomorrow?

_____

"The elevator to success is out of order. You'll have to use the stairs… one step at a time." – Joe Girard

Pretend to Laugh for 10 seconds :)!!!

I am Thankful

1.   I, _____, am_____ for_____,

     because_____

2.   I, _____, am_____ for_____,

     because_____

I am Hardworking

1.   I, _____, am_____

because_____

2.   I, _____, am_____

because_____

Most important tasks of the day?

1._____

2._____

I ate this enhancing super whole food

☐ Eggs ☐ Fish ☐ Beets ☐ Other_____

Nutrition

Rat hairs, maggots, and insects are legally permitted to be in your food. Put INTO YOUR OWN WORDS OR RECOPY_____

I Acknowledge

Three fantastic things that happened today?

1._____

2._____

3._____

I laughed or smiled today because

_____

How will I enhance tomorrow?

_____

"The best way to cheer yourself up is to try to cheer somebody else up." – Mark Twain

Pretend to Laugh for 10 seconds :)!!!

I am Thankful

1.   I, _____, am_____ for_____,

   because_____

2.   I, _____, am_____ for_____,

   because_____

I am Laughing

1.   I, _____, am_____

because_____

2.   I, _____, am_____

because_____

Most important tasks of the day?

   1._____

   2._____

I ate this enhancing super whole food

☐ Eggs ☐ Fish ☐ Orange Peel l ☐ Other_____

Nutrition

McDonald's paid Disney millions so that kids would come to its restaurants.
PUT INTO YOUR OWN WORDS OR
RECOPY_____

I Acknowledge

Three fantastic things that happened today?

1._____

2._____

3._____

I laughed or smiled today because

_____

How will I enhance tomorrow?

_____

"If you don't know where you are going, you might wind up someplace else." – Yogi Berra

Pretend to Laugh for 10 seconds :)!!!

I am Thankful

1.   I, _____, am_____ for_____,

  because_____

2.   I, _____, am_____ for_____,

  because_____

I am Thoughtful

1.   I, _____, am_____

because_____

2.   I, _____, am_____

because_____

Most important tasks of the day?

1._____

2._____

I ate this enhancing super whole food

☐ Eggs ☐ Fish ☐ Lemon ☐ Other_____

Nutrition

Sodium fluoride is a pesticide. PUT INTO YOUR OWN WORDS OR RECOPY_____

Cavemen had no access to bread or McDonald's. PUT INTO YOUR OWN WORDS OR RECOPY_____

I Acknowledge

Three fantastic things that happened today?

1._____

2._____

3._____

I laughed or smiled today because

_____

How will I enhance tomorrow?

_____

"Luck is what you have left over after you give 100 percent."
– Langston Coleman

Pretend to Laugh for 10 seconds :)!!!

I am Thankful

1. I, _____, am_____ for_____,

   because_____

2. I, _____, am_____ for_____,

   because_____

I am Cooking

1. I, _____, am_____

because_____

2. I, _____, am_____

because_____

Most important tasks of the day?

1._____

2._____

I ate this enhancing super whole food

☐ Eggs ☐ Fish ☐ Cherries ☐ Other_____

Nutrition

Lions are not vegetarian. PUT INTO YOUR OWN WORDS OR RECOPY_____

Sugar is less expensive and more accessible than cocaine. PUT INTO YOUR OWN WORDS OR RECOPY_____

I Acknowledge

Three fantastic things that happened today?

1._____

2._____

3._____

I laughed or smiled today because

_____

How will I enhance tomorrow?

_____

"I have not failed. I've just found 10,000 ways that won't work."
Thomas Edison

Pretend to Laugh for 10 seconds :)!!!

I am Thankful

1. I, _____, am_____ for_____,

   because_____

2. I, _____, am_____ for_____,

   because_____

I am Dancing

1. I, _____, am_____

because_____

2. I, _____, am_____

because_____

Most important tasks of the day?

1._____

2._____

I ate this enhancing super whole food

☐ Eggs ☐Fish ☐ Salmon ☐Other_____

Nutrition

Fasting for 12 hours can help you lose weight. PUT INTO YOUR OWN
WORDS OR RECOPY_____

I Acknowledge

Three fantastic things that happened today?

1._____

2._____

3._____

I laughed or smiled today because

_____

How will I enhance tomorrow?

_____

**"We become what we think about most of the time, and that's the
strangest secret."
Earl Nightingale**

Laughter Day!

Pretend to laugh for 10 seconds!

Visualize a family member or close friend Smiling and Laughing

Visualize a colleague Smiling and Laughing

Visualize someone you don't know Smiling and Laughing

Pretend to laugh for 10 seconds

Thank you, Universe, for?

NOTES

Pretend to Laugh for 10 seconds :)!!!

I am Thankful

1.   I, _____, am_____ for_____,

    because_____

2.   I, _____, am_____ for_____,

    because_____

I am Relaxed

1.   I, _____, am_____

because_____

2.   I, _____, am_____

because_____

Most important tasks of the day?

1._____

2._____

I ate this enhancing super whole food

☐ Eggs ☐ Fish ☐ Tuna ☐ Other_____

Nutrition

Consuming sugar induces insulin production. PUT INTO YOUR OWN WORDS OR RECOPY_____

I Acknowledge

Three fantastic things that happened today?

1._____

2._____

3._____

I laughed or smiled today because

_____

How will I enhance tomorrow?

_____

"The No. 1 reason people fail in life is because they listen to their friends, family, and neighbors."
Napoleon Hill

Pretend to Laugh for 10 seconds :)!!!

I am Thankful

1. I, _____, am_____ for_____,

    because_____

2. I, _____, am_____ for_____,

    because_____

I am Swell

1. I, _____, am_____

because_____

2. I, _____, am_____

because_____

Most important tasks of the day?

1._____

2._____

I ate this enhancing super whole food

☐ Eggs ☐ Fish ☐ Sea cucumber ☐ Other_____

Nutrition

Cancer cells ferment sugar to thrive. PUT INTO YOUR OWN WORDS OR
RECOPY_____

Activation of AMPK fuel-sensing enzyme stops cancer growth. PUT INTO
YOUR OWN WORDS OR
RECOPY_____

I Acknowledge

Three fantastic things that happened today?

1._____

2._____

3._____

I laughed or smiled today because

_____

How will I enhance tomorrow?

_____

"What should you do, when you see an endangered animal eating an endangered plant?"
George Carlin

Pretend to Laugh for 10 seconds :)!!!

I am Thankful

1. I, _____ , am_____ for_____ ,

    because_____

2. I, _____ , am_____ for_____ ,

    because_____

I am Fit

1. I, _____ , am_____

because_____

2. I, _____ , am_____

because_____

Most important tasks of the day?

1._____

2._____

I ate this enhancing super whole food

☐ Eggs ☐ Fish ☐ Broccli ☐ Other_____

Nutrition

Many spices and supplements like ginseng activate AMPK.
PUT INTO YOUR OWN WORDS OR
RECOPY_____

Himalayan pink salt contains trace minerals like chromium and selenium.
PUT INTO YOUR OWN WORDS OR
RECOPY_____

I Acknowledge

Three fantastic things that happened today?

1._____

2._____

3._____

I laughed or smiled today because

_____

How will I enhance tomorrow?

_____

"Never keep up with the Joneses. Drag them down to your level; it's cheaper." — Quentin Crisp

Pretend to Laugh for 10 seconds :)!!!

I am Thankful

1. I, _____, am_____ for_____,

because_____

2. I, _____, am_____ for_____,

because_____

I am Toxin-Free

1. I, _____, am_____

because_____

2. I, _____, am_____

because_____

Most important tasks of the day?

1._____

2._____

I ate this enhancing super whole food

☐ Eggs ☐ Fish ☐ Kale ☐ Other_____

Nutrition

Vitamin D supplementation can increase anti-inflammatory cytokine IL-10 by 29%. PUT INTO YOUR OWN WORDS OR RECOPY_____

Some nutrients like curcumin are extremely difficult to absorb. PUT INTO YOUR OWN WORDS OR RECOPY_____

I Acknowledge

Three fantastic things that happened today?

1._____

2._____

3._____

I laughed or smiled today because

_____

How will I enhance tomorrow?

_____

"My parents used to stuff me with candy when I was a kid. M&M's, Jujubes, SweeTarts. I don't think they wanted a child; I think they wanted a piñata."
Wendy Liebman

Pretend to Laugh for 10 seconds :)!!!

I am Thankful

1. I, _____, am_____ for_____,

   because_____

2. I, _____, am_____ for_____,

   because_____

I am Sensational

1. I, _____, am_____

because_____

2. I, _____, am_____

because_____

Most important tasks of the day?

1._____

2._____

I ate this enhancing super whole food

☐ Eggs ☐ Fish ☐ Seeds ☐ Other_____

Nutrition

Consuming eggs reduces proinflammatory marker plasma C-reactive protein. PUT INTO YOUR OWN WORDS OR
RECOPY_____

The liver of a reindeer contains 1000 times more vitamin A than its meat. PUT INTO YOUR OWN WORDS OR
RECOPY_____

I Acknowledge

Three fantastic things that happened today?

1._____

2._____

3._____

I laughed or smiled today because

_____

How will I enhance tomorrow?

_____

"A Canadian psychologist is selling a video that teaches you how to test your dog's IQ. Here's how it works: If you spend $12.99 for the video, your dog is smarter than you."
Jay Leno

Laughter Day!

Pretend to laugh for 10 seconds!

Visualize a family member or close friend Smiling and Laughing

Visualize a colleague Smiling and Laughing

Visualize someone you don't know Smiling and Laughing

Pretend to laugh for 10 seconds

Thank you, Universe, for?

NOTES

Pretend to Laugh for 10 seconds :)!!!

I am Thankful

1. I, _____, am_____ for_____,

   because_____

2. I, _____, am_____ for_____,

   because_____

I am Jokester

1. I, _____, am_____

because_____

2. I, _____, am_____

because_____

Most important tasks of the day?

1._____

2._____

I ate this enhancing super whole food

☐ Eggs ☐ Fish ☐ Cranberries ☐ Other_____

Nutrition

Shrimp are pink because of astaxanthin.
PUT INTO YOUR OWN WORDS OR
RECOPY_____

Vitamin C is responsible for supporting the production of 90% of bone matrix protein.
PUT INTO YOUR OWN WORDS OR
RECOPY_____

I Acknowledge

Three fantastic things that happened today?

1._____

2._____

3._____

I laughed or smiled today because

_____

How will I enhance tomorrow?

_____

"Would you like me to give you a formula for success? It's quite simple, really: Double your rate of failure. You are thinking of failure as the enemy of success. But it isn't at all. You can be discouraged by failure or you can learn from it, so go ahead and make mistakes. Make all you can. Because remember that's where you will find success." Thomas J. Watson

Pretend to Laugh for 10 seconds :)!!!

I am Thankful

1.   I, _____ , am_____ for_____ ,

    because_____

2.   I, _____ , am_____ for_____ ,

    because_____

I am Aroused

1.   I, _____ , am_____

because_____

2.   I, _____ , am_____

because_____

Most important tasks of the day?

    1._____

    2._____

I ate this enhancing super whole food

☐ Eggs ☐ Fish ☐ Rosemary ☐ Other_____

Nutrition

Boiling and chilling potatoes increases the resistance starch in them.
PUT INTO YOUR OWN WORDS OR
RECOPY_____

Pumpkins seeds contain cucurbitacines that activate AMPK.
PUT INTO YOUR OWN WORDS OR
RECOPY_____

I Acknowledge

Three fantastic things that happened today?

1._____

2._____

3._____

I laughed or smiled today because

_____

How will I enhance tomorrow?

_____

"If you don't design your own life plan, chances are you'll fall into someone else's plan. And guess what they have planned for you? Not much." Jim Rohn

Pretend to Laugh for 10 seconds :)!!!

I am Thankful

1. I, _____, am_____ for_____,

    because_____

2. I, _____, am_____ for_____,

    because_____

I am Hunky-dory

1. I, _____, am_____

because_____

2. I, _____, am_____

because_____

Most important tasks of the day?

1._____

2._____

I ate this enhancing super whole food

☐ Eggs ☐ Fish ☐ Basil ☐ Other_____

Nutrition

Pineapple contains the enzyme called bromelian, which improves digestion and increases lactobacillus bacteria. PUT INTO YOUR OWN WORDS OR RECOPY_____

Mushrooms contain immunodulators such as lentinan tht normalize the immune system. PUT INTO YOUR OWN WORDS OR RECOPY_____

I Acknowledge

Three fantastic things that happened today?

1._____

2._____

3._____

I laughed or smiled today because

_____

How will I enhance tomorrow?

_____

"Rarely have I seen a situation where doing less than the other guy is a good strategy."
Jimmy Spithill

Pretend to Laugh for 10 seconds :)!!!

I am Thankful

1. I, _____, am_____ for_____,

    because_____

2. I, _____, am_____ for_____,

    because_____

I am a Champion

1. I, _____, am_____

because_____

2. I, _____, am_____

because_____

Most important tasks of the day?

1._____

2._____

I ate this enhancing super whole food

☐ Eggs ☐ Fish ☐ Kale ☐ Other_____

Nutrition

Potatoes were domesticated 8000 years ago by the Incan Empire. PUT INTO YOUR OWN WORDS OR
RECOPY_____

The difference between black tea and green tea is how the tea leaves are processed. PUT INTO YOUR OWN WORDS OR
RECOPY_____

I Acknowledge

Three fantastic things that happened today?

1._____

2._____

3._____

I laughed or smiled today because

_____

How will I enhance tomorrow?

_____

"Though no one can go back and make a brand-new start, anyone can start from now and make a brand-new ending."
Carl Bard

Pretend to Laugh for 10 seconds :)!!!

I am Thankful

1. I, _____, am_____ for_____,

   because_____

2. I, _____, am_____ for_____,

   because_____

I am Flirtatious

1. I, _____, am_____

because_____

2. I, _____, am_____

because_____

Most important tasks of the day?

1._____

2._____

I ate this enhancing super whole food

☐ Eggs ☐ Fish ☐ Yes, Kale ☐ Other_____

Nutrition

The Japanese consume the most iodine in the world, over 10 times the RDI.
PUT INTO YOUR OWN WORDS OR
RECOPY_____

2-mins of powering posing could increase your testosterone. PUT INTO
YOUR OWN WORDS OR
RECOPY_____

I Acknowledge

Three fantastic things that happened today?

1._____

2._____

3._____

I laughed or smiled today because

_____

How will I enhance tomorrow?

_____

_____

**"Success is walking from failure to failure with no loss of
enthusiasm."
Winston Churchill**

Pretend to Laugh for 10 seconds :)!!!

I am Thankful

1. I, _____, am_____ for_____,

    because_____

2. I, _____, am_____ for_____,

    because_____

I am so Attractive

1. I, _____, am_____

because_____

2. I, _____, am_____

because_____

Most important tasks of the day?

    1._____

    2._____

I ate this enhancing super whole food

☐ Eggs ☐Fish ☐ Kale, again ☐Other_____

Nutrition

Real and fabricated laughing can lower cortisol levels. PUT INTO YOUR OWN WORDS OR RECOPY

Meditation can increase the release of dopamine. PUT INTO YOUR OWN WORDS OR RECOPY_____

I Acknowledge

Three fantastic things that happened today?

1._____

2._____

3._____

I laughed or smiled today because

_____

How will I enhance tomorrow?

_____

"The key to success is not through achievement, but through enthusiasm." – Malcolm Forbes

Pretend to Laugh for 10 seconds :)!!!

I am Thankful

1.   I, _____, am_____ for_____,

    because_____

2.   I, _____, am_____ for_____,

    because_____

I am Confident

1.   I, _____, am_____

because_____

2.   I, _____, am_____

because_____

Most important tasks of the day?

1._____

2._____

I ate this enhancing super whole food

☐ Eggs ☐ Fish ☐ Miso ☐ Other_____

Nutrition

According to the Journal of American Medical association, in 2010, there were 16, 451 unintentional pharmaceutical-related overdose deaths in the U.S. PUT INTO YOUR OWN WORDS OR RECOPY_____

I Acknowledge

Three fantastic things that happened today?

1._____

2._____

3._____

I laughed or smiled today because

_____

How will I enhance tomorrow?

_____

"I've often said, the only thing standing between me and greatness is me." - Woody Allen

Pretend to Laugh for 10 seconds :)!!!

I am Thankful

1.   I, _____ , am_____ for_____ ,

   because_____

2.   I, _____ , am_____ for_____ ,

   because_____

I am Muscular

1.   I, _____ , am_____

because_____

2.   I, _____ , am_____

because_____

Most important tasks of the day?

1._____

2._____

I ate this enhancing super whole food

☐ Eggs ☐Fish ☐ Beets ☐Other_____

Nutrition

According to the American Nutrition Association, nonsteroidal anti-inflammatory drugs (NSAIDS) like aspirin cause over 100, 000 Americans to be hospitalized for gastrointestinal complications. PUT INTO YOUR OWN WORDS OR RECOPY_____

I Acknowledge

Three fantastic things that happened today?

1._____

2._____

3._____

I laughed or smiled today because

_____

How will I enhance tomorrow?

_____

"Life is very interesting. In the end, some of your greatest pains become your greatest strengths." —Drew Barrymore

Laughter Day!

Pretend to laugh for 10 seconds!

Visualize a family member or close friend Smiling and Laughing

Visualize a colleague Smiling and Laughing

Visualize someone you don't know Smiling and Laughing

Pretend to laugh for 10 seconds

Thank you, Universe, for?

NOTES

Pretend to Laugh for 10 seconds :)!!!

I am Thankful

1. I, _____, am_____ for_____,

    because_____

2. I, _____, am_____ for_____,

    because_____

I am Rich

1. I, _____, am_____

because_____

2. I, _____, am_____

because_____

Most important tasks of the day?

1._____

2._____

I ate this enhancing super whole food

☐ Eggs ☐ Fish ☐ Olive Oil ☐ Other_____

Nutrition

According to Dr. Duke's phytochemical database, an apple contains 574 chemicals. PUT INTO YOUR OWN WORDS OR
RECOPY_____

You can make your own probiotics by putting veggies in jar filled water and a little salt. PUT INTO YOUR OWN WORDS OR
RECOPY_____

I Acknowledge

Three fantastic things that happened today?

1._____

2._____

3._____

I laughed or smiled today because

_____

How will I enhance tomorrow?

_____

"I'm convinced that about half of what separates the successful entrepreneurs from the non-successful ones is pure perseverance."
Steve Jobs

Pretend to Laugh for 10 seconds :)!!!

I am Thankful

1.   I, _____, am_____ for_____,

    because_____

2.   I, _____, am_____ for_____,

    because_____

I am Really Rich

1.   I, _____, am_____

because_____

2.   I, _____, am_____

because_____

Most important tasks of the day?

1._____

2._____

I ate this enhancing super whole food

☐ Eggs ☐ Fish ☐ Coconut Oil ☐ Other_____

Nutrition

According to Torstar News Service investigation, "drug companies routinely host and fund these dinners at upscale restaurants as training events for family doctors." PUT INTO YOUR OWN WORDS OR
RECOPY_____

In Canada, doctors can attend industry-sponsored events for purposes of continuing their medical education to keep their medical license. PUT INTO YOUR OWN WORDS OR
RECOPY_____

I Acknowledge

Three fantastic things that happened today?

1._____

2._____

3._____

I laughed or smiled today because

_____

How will I enhance tomorrow?

_____

"Successful people tend to become more successful because they are always thinking about their successes." - Brian Tracy

Pretend to Laugh for 10 seconds :)!!!

I am Thankful

1.   I, _____, am_____ for_____,

   because_____

2.   I, _____, am_____ for_____,

   because_____

I am Smart

1.   I, _____, am_____

because_____

2.   I, _____, am_____

because_____

Most important tasks of the day?

   1._____

   2._____

I ate this enhancing super whole food

☐ Eggs ☐ Fish ☐ Olive Oil ☐ Other_____

Nutrition

According to a U.S medical school national survey, in 2010, only 25% of medical schools required a dedicated nutrition course. PUT INTO YOUR OWN WORDS OR
RECOPY_____

According to a U.S medical school national survey, in 2010, average nutrition instruction was 19.6 hours or less than 2 credits. PUT INTO YOUR OWN WORDS OR RECOPY_____

I Acknowledge

Three fantastic things that happened today?

1._____

2._____

3._____

I laughed or smiled today because

_____

How will I enhance tomorrow?

_____

"Team work is important; it helps to put the blame on someone else."

Pretend to Laugh for 10 seconds :)!!!

I am Thankful

1.   I, _____, am_____ for_____,

because_____

2.   I, _____, am_____ for_____,

because_____

I am Jolly

1.   I, _____, am_____

because_____

2.   I, _____, am_____

because_____

Most important tasks of the day?

1._____

2._____

I ate this enhancing super whole food

☐ Eggs ☐ Fish ☐ Kale ☐ Other_____

Nutrition

Persistent organic pollutants (POPs), pesticides, heavy metals, and other contaminants accumulate in human milk. PUT INTO YOUR OWN WORDS OR RECOPY_____

I Acknowledge

Three fantastic things that happened today?

1._____

2._____

3._____

I laughed or smiled today because

_____

How will I enhance tomorrow?

_____

"If I had a dollar for every girl that found me unattractive, they would eventually find me attractive."

Pretend to Laugh for 10 seconds :)!!!

I am Thankful

1. I, _____, am_____ for_____,

   because_____

2. I, _____, am_____ for_____,

   because_____

I am Effective

1. I, _____, am_____

   because_____

2. I, _____, am_____

   because_____

Most important tasks of the day?

1._____

2._____

I ate this enhancing super whole food

☐ Eggs ☐ Fish ☐ Peppers ☐ Other_____

Nutrition

Baking soda supplementation is a proven effective cancer treatment in mice. PUT INTO YOUR OWN WORDS OR RECOPY_____

Sodium bicarbonate intake improves high-intensity intermittent exercise performance in trained young men. PUT INTO YOUR OWN WORDS OR RECOPY_____

I Acknowledge

Three fantastic things that happened today?

1._____

2._____

3._____

I laughed or smiled today because

_____

How will I enhance tomorrow?

_____

"When wearing a bikini, women reveal 90 % of their body... men are so polite they only look at the covered parts."

Laughter Day!

Pretend to laugh for 10 seconds!

Visualize a family member or close friend Smiling and Laughing

Visualize a colleague Smiling and Laughing

Visualize someone you don't know Smiling and Laughing

Pretend to laugh for 10 seconds

Thank you, Universe, for?

NOTES

Pretend to Laugh for 10 seconds :)!!!

I am Thankful

1. I, _____, am_____ for_____,

   because_____

2. I, _____, am_____ for_____,

   because_____

I am Singing

1. I, _____, am_____

because_____

2. I, _____, am_____

because_____

Most important tasks of the day?

1._____

2._____

I ate this enhancing super whole food

☐ Eggs ☐ Fish ☐ Red Pepper ☐ Other_____

Nutrition

Supplementation with Gotu kola is proven to heal skin problems like burns and stretch marks.   PUT INTO YOUR OWN WORDS OR RECOPY_____

Fat is also known as adipose tissue. Fat-soluble toxins accumulate and are stored in fat cells. PUT INTO YOUR OWN WORDS OR RECOPY_____

I Acknowledge

Three fantastic things that happened today?

1._____

2._____

3._____

I laughed or smiled today because

_____

How will I enhance tomorrow?

_____

"Life is all about perspective. The sinking of the Titanic was a miracle to the lobsters in the ship's kitchen."

Pretend to Laugh for 10 seconds :)!!!

I am Thankful

1. I, _____, am_____ for_____,

   because_____

2. I, _____, am_____ for_____,

   because_____

I am Nutrient-dense

1. I, _____, am_____

because_____

2. I, _____, am_____

because_____

Most important tasks of the day?

1._____

2._____

I ate this enhancing super whole food

☐ Eggs ☐ Fish ☐ Black Pepper ☐ Other_____

Nutrition

The panama disease caused the Gros Michael variety of banana to be replaced by the seedless Cavendish banana. PUT INTO YOUR OWN WORDS OR
RECOPY_____

Potatoes were brought to Europe via Spain from South America in 1536. PUT INTO YOUR OWN WORDS OR
RECOPY_____

I Acknowledge

Three fantastic things that happened today?

1._____

2._____

3._____

I laughed or smiled today because

_____

How will I enhance tomorrow?

_____

"When my boss asked me who is the stupid one, me or him? I told him everyone knows he doesn't hire stupid people."

Pretend to Laugh for 10 seconds :)!!!

I am Thankful

1.   I, _____, am_____ for_____,

    because_____

2.   I, _____, am_____ for_____,

    because_____

I am Fit

1.   I, _____, am_____

because_____

2.   I, _____, am_____

because_____

Most important tasks of the day?

1._____

2._____

I ate this enhancing super whole food

☐ Eggs ☐ Fish ☐ Kalel ☐ Other_____

Nutrition

The potato was domesticated in South America over 7000 years ago. PUT INTO YOUR OWN WORDS OR RECOPY_____

Olive oil is comprised of mainly oleic acid (monounsaturated Omega-9 fatty acid) PUT INTO YOUR OWN WORDS OR RECOPY_____

I Acknowledge

Three fantastic things that happened today?

1._____

2._____

3._____

I laughed or smiled today because

_____

How will I enhance tomorrow?

_____

"I'm great at multitasking. I can waste time, be unproductive, and procrastinate all at once."

Pretend to Laugh for 10 seconds :)!!!

I am Thankful

1.   I, _____, am_____ for_____,

    because_____

2.   I, _____, am_____ for_____,

    because_____

I am Passionate

1.   I, _____, am_____

because_____

2.   I, _____, am_____

because_____

Most important tasks of the day?

1._____

2._____

I ate this enhancing super whole food

☐ Eggs ☐ Fish ☐ Kale ☐ Other_____

Nutrition

Caffeine is natural insecticide produced by coffee and tea plants. PUT INTO YOUR OWN WORDS OR
RECOPY_____

There are 4 calories in a gram of sugar, 4 calories in a gram of protein and 9 calories in a gram of fat. PUT INTO YOUR OWN WORDS OR
RECOPY_____

I Acknowledge

Three fantastic things that happened today?

1._____

2._____

3._____

I laughed or smiled today because

_____

How will I enhance tomorrow?

_____

"Alcohol is a perfect solvent: It dissolves marriages, families and careers."

Pretend to Laugh for 10 seconds :)!!!

I am Thankful

1.   I, _____, am_____ for_____,

   because_____

2.   I, _____, am_____ for_____,

   because_____

I am Charming

1.   I, _____, am_____

because_____

2.   I, _____, am_____

because_____

Most important tasks of the day?

1._____

2._____

I ate this enhancing super whole food

☐ Eggs ☐ Fish ☐ Lemon ☐ Other_____

Nutrition

France gave up its claim for most of North America to Britain in 1763, in order to secure the sugar producing West Indian islands. PUT INTO YOUR OWN WORDS OR
RECOPY_____

In order to reduce its trade deficit with China around 1820s, Britain illegally sold Indian opium to the Chinese. Britain later invaded China because the Chinese Emperor ordered the destruction of British owned opium cargo. PUT INTO YOUR OWN WORDS OR
RECOPY_____

I Acknowledge

Three fantastic things that happened today?

1._____

2._____

3._____

I laughed or smiled today because

_____

How will I enhance tomorrow?

_____

"Intelligence is like an underwear. It is important that you have it, but not necessary that you show it off."

Pretend to Laugh for 10 seconds :)!!!

I am Thankful

1.   I, _____, am_____ for_____,

because_____

2.   I, _____, am_____ for_____,

because_____

I am Smiling

1.   I, _____, am_____

because_____

2.   I, _____, am_____

because_____

Most important tasks of the day?

1._____

2._____

I ate this enhancing super whole food

☐ Eggs ☐Fish ☐ Pear ☐Other_____

Nutrition

In 2011, the State of Connecticut banned BPA use in receipts. PUT INTO YOUR OWN WORDS OR
RECOPY_____

It is illegal in America for humans to consume non-prescribed anabolic steroids. However, it is legal in America to eat an animal that has been treated with anabolic steroids. PUT INTO YOUR OWN WORDS OR
RECOPY_____

I Acknowledge

Three fantastic things that happened today?

1._____

2._____

3._____

I laughed or smiled today because

_____

How will I enhance tomorrow?

_____

"I changed my password to 'incorrect.' So, whenever I forget what it is, the computer will say 'Your password is incorrect.'"

Pretend to Laugh for 10 seconds :)!!!

I am Thankful

1.   I, _____, am_____ for_____,

because_____

2.   I, _____, am_____ for_____,

because_____

I am Laughing

1.   I, _____, am_____

because_____

2.   I, _____, am_____

because_____

Most important tasks of the day?

1._____

2._____

I ate this enhancing super whole food

☐ Eggs ☐ Fish ☐ Celery ☐ Other_____

Nutrition

A healthy animal does not need antibiotics to survive. PUT INTO YOUR OWN WORDS OR

RECOPY_____

To protect its citizens, Europe banned American hormone-filled meat. In response, America took Europe to the World Trade Organization. As a result, the WTO ordered Europe to pay $100 million per year of the Ban. PUT INTO YOUR OWN WORDS OR

RECOPY_____

I Acknowledge

Three fantastic things that happened today?

1._____

2._____

3._____

I laughed or smiled today because

_____

How will I enhance tomorrow?

_____

"Improve your memory by doing unforgettable things."

<u>Laughter Day!</u>

Pretend to laugh for 10 seconds!

Visualize a family member or close friend Smiling and Laughing

Visualize a colleague Smiling and Laughing

Visualize someone you don't know Smiling and Laughing

Pretend to laugh for 10 seconds

Thank you, Universe, for?

NOTES

Pretend to Laugh for 10 seconds :)!!!

I am Thankful

1. I, _____, am _____ for _____,

because_____

2. I, _____, am _____ for _____,

because_____

I am Toxin-Free

1. I, _____, am _____

because_____

2. I, _____, am _____

because_____

Most important tasks of the day?

1._____

2._____

I ate this enhancing super whole food

☐ Eggs ☐ Fish ☐ Kale ☐ Other_____

Nutrition

In 1981, the Europe Union prohibited the use of substances having a hormonal action for growth promotion in farm animals. Examples of these growth promoters included were oestradiol 17ß, testosterone, progesterone, zeranol, trenbolone acetate and melengestrol acetate (MGA). PUT INTO YOUR OWN WORDS OR
RECOPY_____

Organ meats contain more Coenzyme Q10 than non-organ meats. PUT INTO YOUR OWN WORDS OR
RECOPY_____ _____

I Acknowledge

Three fantastic things that happened today?

1._____

2._____

3._____

I laughed or smiled today because

_____

How will I enhance tomorrow?

_____

"Any married man should forget his mistakes, there's no use in two people remembering the same thing."

Pretend to Laugh for 10 seconds :)!!!

I am Thankful

1. I, _____, am_____ for_____,

   because_____

2. I, _____, am_____ for_____,

   because_____

I am Muscular

1. I, _____, am_____

because_____

2. I, _____, am_____

because_____

Most important tasks of the day?

1._____

2._____

I ate this enhancing super whole food

☐ Eggs ☐ Fish ☐ Salmon ☐ Other_____

Nutrition

Glutamine supplementation can aid the gut microbiome and induce weight-loss. PUT INTO YOUR OWN WORDS OR RECOPY_____ _____.

The long-chain omega-3 fatty acids, eicosapentaenoic acid (EPA) and docosahexaenoic acid (DHA), can be synthesized from ALA, but due to low conversion efficiency, it is recommended to obtain EPA and DHA from additional sources.

I Acknowledge

Three fantastic things that happened today?

1._____

2._____

3._____

I laughed or smiled today because

_____

How will I enhance tomorrow?

_____

"The trouble with being punctual is that nobody's there to appreciate it."
- Franklin P. Jones

Pretend to Laugh for 10 seconds :)!!!

I am Thankful

1. I, _____, am_____ for_____,

    because_____

2. I, _____, am_____ for_____,

    because_____

I am Fashion Savvy

1. I, _____, am_____

because_____

2. I, _____, am_____

because_____

Most important tasks of the day?

1._____

2._____

I ate this enhancing super whole food

☐ Eggs ☐ Fish ☐ Pear ☐ Other_____

Nutrition

Linoleic acid (LA), an omega-6 fatty acid, and α-linolenic acid (ALA), an omega-3 fatty acid, are considered essential fatty acids (EFA) because they cannot be synthesized by humans. PUT INTO YOUR OWN WORDS OR RECOPY_____

Arachidonic acid: Animals, but not plants, can convert LA to AA. Therefore, AA is present in small amounts in meat, poultry, and eggs. PUT INTO YOUR OWN WORDS OR RECOPY_____

I Acknowledge

Three fantastic things that happened today?

1._____

2._____

3._____

I laughed or smiled today because

_____

How will I enhance tomorrow?

_____

"Good advice is something a man gives when he is too old to set a bad example."
- La Rochefoucald

Pretend to Laugh for 10 seconds :)!!!

I am Thankful

1.   I, _____, am_____ for_____,

    because_____

2.   I, _____, am_____ for_____,

    because_____

I am Strong

1.   I, _____, am_____

because_____

2.   I, _____, am_____

because_____

Most important tasks of the day?

    1._____

    2._____

I ate this enhancing super whole food

☐ Eggs ☐ Fish ☐ Olive Oil ☐ Other_____

Nutrition

Studies of ALA metabolism in healthy young men indicate that approximately 8% of dietary ALA is converted to EPA and 0-4% is converted to DHA. PUT INTO YOUR OWN WORDS OR
RECOPY_____

Arachidonic acid is a polyunsaturated fatty acid present in phospholipids (especially phosphatidylethanolamine, phosphatidylcholine, and phosphatidylinositides) of membranes of the body's cells, and is abundant in the brain, muscles, and liver. PUT INTO YOUR OWN WORDS OR
RECOPY_____

I Acknowledge

Three fantastic things that happened today?

1._____

2._____

3._____

I laughed or smiled today because

_____

How will I enhance tomorrow?

_____

"Hating people is like burning down your own home to get rid of a rat."
- Harry Emerson Fosdick

Pretend to Laugh for 10 seconds :)!!!

I am Thankful

1.   I, _____, am_____ for_____,

   because_____

2.   I, _____, am_____ for_____,

   because_____

I am Sexual

1.   I, _____, am_____

because_____

2.   I, _____, am_____

because_____

Most important tasks of the day?

   1._____

   2._____

I ate this enhancing super whole food

☐ Eggs ☐Fish ☐ Apple ☐Other_____

Nutrition

To produce DNA, your body needs vitamin B9 (Folate). Good sources of folate include Lentils, garbanzo beans and spinach. PUT INTO YOUR OWN WORDS OR RECOPY_____

_____

Parsley derives its name from the Greek word meaning "rock celery." PUT INTO YOUR OWN WORDS OR RECOPY_____ _____

I Acknowledge

Three fantastic things that happened today?

1._____

2._____

3._____

I laughed or smiled today because

_____

How will I enhance tomorrow?

_____

"Laughter is a weapon of mass construction."
- Kat Caverly

Pretend to Laugh for 10 seconds :)!!!

I am Thankful

1.   I, _____, am_____ for_____,

   because_____

2.   I, _____, am_____ for_____,

   because_____

I am Beautiful

1.   I, _____, am_____

because_____

2.   I, _____, am_____

because_____

Most important tasks of the day?

   1._____

   2._____

I ate this enhancing super whole food

☐ Eggs ☐ Fish ☐ Super Kale ☐ Other_____

Nutrition

Manganese found in cloves, oats and brown rice, is necessary for the production of collagen and skin. PUT INTO YOUR OWN WORDS OR RECOPY_____ _____

Consuming oats that contain avenanthramides reduces inflammation. PUT INTO YOUR OWN WORDS OR RECOPY_____ _____

I Acknowledge

Three fantastic things that happened today?

1._____

2._____

3._____

I laughed or smiled today because

_____

How will I enhance tomorrow?

_____

"There are basically two types of people. People who accomplish things, and people who claim to have accomplished things. The first group is less crowded."
- Mark Twain

<u>Laughter Day!</u>

Pretend to laugh for 10 seconds!

Visualize a family member or close friend Smiling and Laughing

Visualize a colleague Smiling and Laughing

Visualize someone you don't know Smiling and Laughing

Pretend to laugh for 10 seconds

Thank you, Universe, for?

<u>NOTES</u>

Pretend to Laugh for 10 seconds :)!!!

I am Thankful

1.   I, _____, am_____ for_____,

  because_____

2.   I, _____, am_____ for_____,

  because_____

I am Rich

1.   I, _____, am_____

because_____

2.   I, _____, am_____

because_____

Most important tasks of the day?

1._____

2._____

I ate this enhancing super whole food

☐ Eggs ☐ Fish ☐ Spinach ☐ Other_____

Nutrition

Over 50% of coconut oil is made up of medium-chained fatty acids. PUT INTO YOUR OWN WORDS OR
RECOPY_____ _____

Medium-chained fatty acids have been proven to improve cognitive function. PUT INTO YOUR OWN WORDS OR
RECOPY_____ _____

I Acknowledge

Three fantastic things that happened today?

1._____

2._____

3._____

I laughed or smiled today because

_____

How will I enhance tomorrow?

_____

"Change is not a four-letter word… but often your reaction to it is!"
- Jeffrey Gitomer

Pretend to Laugh for 10 seconds :)!!!

I am Thankful

1. I, _____, am_____ for_____,

   because_____

2. I, _____, am_____ for_____,

   because_____

I am Really Fit

1. I, _____, am_____

because_____

2. I, _____, am_____

because_____

Most important tasks of the day?

1._____

2._____

I ate this enhancing super whole food

☐ Eggs ☐ Fish ☐ Oatmeal ☐ Other_____

Nutrition

Gut microbiota can produce short-chained fatty acids like butyrate, propionic and acetic acid from fiber and resistant starch. Butyrate can protect the brain and enhance plasticity. PUT INTO YOUR OWN WORDS OR RECOPY_____ _____

Consuming deep-fried food has been proven to destroy gut histological structure and unbalance the microbiota profile. PUT INTO YOUR OWN WORDS OR RECOPY_____

I Acknowledge

Three fantastic things that happened today?

1._____

2._____

3._____

I laughed or smiled today because

_____

How will I enhance tomorrow?

_____

"If you're going to be thinking, you may as well think big."
-Donald Trump

Laughter Day!

Pretend to laugh for 10 seconds!

Visualize a family member or close friend Smiling and Laughing

Visualize a colleague Smiling and Laughing

Visualize someone you don't know Smiling and Laughing

Pretend to laugh for 10 seconds

Thank you, Universe, for?

NOTES

www.ingramcontent.com/pod-product-compliance
Lightning Source LLC
Chambersburg PA
CBHW081359270326
41930CB00015B/3355